# DAHLONEGA

# Dahlonega

## A Brief History

Anne Dismukes Amerson

Published by The History Press
Charleston, SC 29403
www.historypress.net



*Front cover:* The 1836 Lumpkin County Courthouse as it appeared circa 1880. *Courtesy of the Georgia Department of Archives and History.*

*Back cover:* R.D. Hogue, owner of the Josephine Mine, was featured in a newsreel entitled "Gold Panning as a Hobby," filmed in Dahlonega in 1951. *Courtesy of the author.*

First published 2006

Manufactured in the United States

ISBN-10 1.59629.130.3
ISBN-13 978.1.54020.410.3

Library of Congress Cataloging-in-Publication Data

Amerson, Anne.
Dahlonega, Georgia : a brief history / Anne Amerson.
p. cm.
Includes bibliographical references and index.
ISBN-13: 978-1-54020-410-3 (alk. paper)
ISBN-10: 1-59629-130-3 (alk. paper)
1. Dahlonega (Ga.)--History. 2. Dahlonega (Ga.)--Economic conditions. 3. Dahlonega (Ga.)--Gold discoveries. 4. Gold mines and mining--Georgia--Dahlonega--History. I. Title.
F294.D13A445 2006
2006023904

# Contents

# Preface

When it was time to select a picture for the cover of this book, I considered many but found only one that was representative of Dahlonega in both past and present. Built in 1836 when the Cherokees were still here and Dahlonega was little more than a rough gold mining camp, the stately Lumpkin County Courthouse has been the focal point of local history for one hundred and seventy years.

In addition to its designated use as a court of justice, the historic old building was a gathering place for many community meetings, and its walls resonated with the rhetoric of long and passionate speeches. It saw use as a college classroom, a market and a hospital. It was the scene of marriages, fights and even a murder. It took bullets from more than one gun battle in its earlier days. A few slaves were sold on its steps. Ammunition was stored and prisoners were restrained within its walls during the Civil War.

The Lumpkin County Courthouse was featured in the September 21, 1942 issue of *Life* magazine. A typical court week was depicted with numerous photographs of the building as well as the people who dispensed and received justice within its walls.

When a new and larger facility was built in the mid-1960s, the fate of the shabby old courthouse hung in the balance. At a time when it was fashionable to tear down the old and replace it with the new, some people wanted the outmoded structure demolished to make more room for parking on the Public Square. Happily, those who favored preservation prevailed.

The historic structure—the oldest surviving courthouse in Georgia—has been in use since 1967 as the Dahlonega Gold Museum, which is today the second most visited historic site in Georgia. Visitors come from all over the country and world to learn about the gold rush that brought Dahlonega into being. The museum's major attraction is its complete set of rare gold coins made at the United States Mint that operated in Dahlonega from 1838 to 1861.

In more recent times, the history of Dahlonega has been depicted in an artistic creation called a Maibaum, or History Tree, that stands in the City Park just north of the Public Square. It is a twenty-nine-foot metal pole with branches of plate steel that artists have cut out to create silhouettes of scenes from the community's past.

2000

# Preface

The History Tree's lowest branch shows prehistoric wildlife and virgin forest before the arrival of humans. The next level portrays Native Americans hunting and fishing, while the third tier announces the arrival of early settlers with their log cabins and plows.

The discovery of gold is depicted on the fourth level by men using gold pans and hydraulic cannons, while the fifth tier shows the Dahlonega Branch Mint, occupying Federal soldiers following the Civil War, a gold stamp mill, the courthouse and the 1884 old jail.

North Georgia College is represented in level six by its hallmark steeple and by cadets serving in five wars. The top branch depicts the Dahlonega Public Square today, represented by the Welcome Center and visitors strolling on the sidewalks and sitting on benches. The tree, which was commissioned for Dahlonega's Golden Millennium Celebration, is capped by the date 2000.

The History Tree's branches present an artistic outline of events that created and shaped the development and growth of this unique community. The purpose of this book is to flesh out the outline in a narrative way that readers will hopefully find interesting, entertaining and informative.

*Opposite:* This twenty-nine-foot metal History Tree depicting local events in seven tiers was commissioned and dedicated as part of Dahlonega's Golden Millennium Celebration. *Courtesy of the author.*

# Acknowledgements

A number of people have contributed to the writing of this book by sharing both information and photographs. Thanks to their input, the contents are much more accurate and complete than they would otherwise have been.

My deepest thanks go to Debra Capponi, information specialist at the Lumpkin County Library; Hal Williams at the Chamber of Commerce Welcome Center; Annette Lee at North Georgia College & State University; Robin Glass and Teresa Krummel at the Dahlonega Gold Museum; Bill Kinsland of Hometown Books; and, last but not least, retired postmaster Jimmy Anderson, who has probably forgotten more about Dahlonega and Lumpkin County than I'll ever learn.

The technical aspects of writing have changed phenomenally since the days when I did my composing at a manual typewriter. I'm appreciative of those who have expedited the writing process with those wonderful but temperamental machines called computers, but I'd probably have to go back to a typewriter without my in-house computer troubleshooter—aka my husband Amos. These acknowledgements would not be complete without thanking him for fifty years of love and support.

I think it is appropriate also to acknowledge all the people who lived their lives in ways that created Dahlonega's unique and fascinating history. If it were not for them, this book would not exist.

# 1

# Dahlonega: Site of the First Major Gold Rush in the United States

## Benjamin Parks Kicked Up a Gold-Bearing Rock

A young man named Benjamin Parks moved to Hall County with his family shortly after it was created in 1818 from land ceded by the Cherokees. Although he lived on the east side of the Chestatee River—the boundary line between Hall County and the Cherokee Nation—Parks was friendly with the Indians and frequently crossed the river to visit with them. In later years he was quoted as saying, "We always treated them right, and they did the same by us."

Parks reportedly fell in love with the daughter of a Cherokee chief but decided not to marry her because his family would not accept the match. "Our children would have had no nation," he explained, "so I did not marry her, but, dear me, how beautiful she was!"

According to an article published in the *Atlanta Constitution* in 1894, based upon an interview with Parks when he was ninety-two, he had been deer hunting just east of the Chestatee when he kicked up a rock that caught his eye. Examining it closely and suspecting that it might contain gold, young Ben went to Robert O'Barr, owner of the property and pastor of Yellow Creek Baptist Church, where Parks himself was a member.

"I told him that I thought I could find gold on his place if he would give me a lease of it," Parks related. "He laughed, as though he did not believe me, and consented. So, a lease for forty years was written out, the consideration of which was, that I was to give him one-fourth of the gold mined." Parks recalled that when he returned to the spot with a pan and turned over the earth, "it looked like the yellow of an egg. It was more than my eyes could believe."

When O'Barr learned that Parks had struck it rich on his land, he was not content with his one-fourth share and attempted to revoke the lease. When that failed, he sold the land (Parks was leasing only the mineral rights) to a Judge Underwood, who in turn sold it to Senator John C. Calhoun of South Carolina.

"Senator Calhoun wanted to buy my lease, and I sold it for what I thought was a good price," Parks told the *Constitution* reporter. "The very first month after the sale, he took out 24,000 pennyweights of gold, and then I was inclined to be as mad with him, as O'Barr had been with me. But that is the peculiarity of gold mining...It is just like gambling—all luck."

Benjamin Parks is credited with being the first to discover gold in north Georgia when he kicked up a gold-bearing rock. *Courtesy of the author.*

According to Parks, his discovery was made in 1828, but even though his mind was obviously still keen when he was interviewed, his memory may have been faulty on some of the details. The lease he signed with Robert O'Barr was not dated until September 12, 1829. It is possible, however, that Parks may not have realized what he had found until an article appeared in a Milledgeville newspaper on August 1, 1829, describing the recent discovery of gold in Habersham County in north Georgia.

Parks apparently overestimated the amount of John C. Calhoun's initial mining success. A pennyweight is one-twentieth of an ounce, and with gold selling for $20 an ounce, his find would have been $24,000, yet Calhoun's first deposit at the U.S. Mint in Philadelphia was valued at only $603.93. The Calhoun mine, however, later became one of the richest and most famous mines in the area.

By the fall of 1829, many newspapers across the state were publishing articles about the riches to be found in Georgia's gold region and men from all walks of life soon flocked to the mountains with gold pans in hand. It was reported that four thousand miners were washing the sands of Yahoola Creek by June of 1830.

"The news got abroad, and such excitement you never saw," Parks reminisced. "It seemed...as if the whole world must have heard of it, for men came from every state I had ever heard of. They came afoot, on horseback and in wagons, acting more like crazy men than anything else. All the way, from where Dahlonega now stands to Nuckollsville, there were men panning out of the branches, and making holes in the hillsides."

## MINERS INVENTED METHODS OF EXTRACTING GOLD

Initially, all gold was found by "placer" or "deposit" mining—using pans to wash ore shoveled up from the beds of streams and branches. Early miners swirled their pans to wash out sand and gravel until only the gold remained. Because the precious metal was heavier than the other materials, it sank to the bottom and was not lost if a miner was skilled with the technique. When gold was still plentiful, miners frequently found numerous flakes, grains and even nuggets of shining "color" in their pans. The smaller particles were frequently poked into the hollows of goose quills for safekeeping.

When gold mining was temporarily suspended, first by the Federal government in 1830 and shortly thereafter by the state of Georgia, troops were sent to patrol the area. Anyone found mining was arrested or at least escorted out of the area with a stern warning not to return. However, men crazed with gold fever soon found a way to continue their search without fear of the soldiers' dawn-to-dusk raids. From camps on the Hall County side of the Chestatee River, they sneaked across the river at night and filled large sacks with ore from areas known to contain rich deposits. Carrying the heavy bags back across the Chestatee to Hall County, they spent the next day panning out the contents in safety.

Seeking ways to process more ore in the course of a day, miners invented several devices to separate gold from the sand in which it was found. These included the hollow gum rocker, the cradle rocker and the sluice box. These containers were filled with ore and agitated while being washed with a flow of water, causing the gold to sink to the bottom and be caught on riffle bars, while the detritus was washed out the other end.

A miner agitates ore in a sluice box to cause the gold to settle to the bottom and be caught on riffle bars. *Courtesy of the Georgia Department of Archives and History.*

In time, miners realized that the placer gold deposits did not originate in streams but had eroded down from the hillsides over time. As a result they began tunneling into slopes in search of vein gold. Because this gold was encased in hard rock, the ore had to be crushed to release the precious metal from the surrounding quartz. Small rocks could be hand crushed using a cast-iron mortar and pestle.

A very simple early crushing or "stamping" device was made by suspending a six-foot section of an oak log from a bent-over sapling. Grasping handles attached to the side, a man could bring the log down repeatedly upon gold-bearing rocks with considerable force, while the spring in the tree lifted the log between blows. When the repeated pounding had reduced the rock to fine sand, it was panned to recover the gold.

Mining companies with more capital to invest than individual miners built large stamp mills consisting of ten or more iron stamps, each weighing five hundred or more pounds. The stamping action of these mills was extremely noisy and could be heard for miles. Men who regularly shoveled ore beneath the stamps frequently lost much of their hearing.

The crushed ore then went into a sluice box to be washed. The gold, being heavier, fell to the bottom, where it was caught on copper plates coated with mercury to attract the fine particles. Periodically, the mill was shut down for cleanup, which consisted of scraping the gold-bearing mercury from the riffled plates. This amalgam was put into an iron container called a retort and heated in the blacksmith's forge until the mercury boiled out. In describing how the gold melted and ran together, one old miner said it came out looking "like a half-pound of yellow butter."

## DREDGE BOATS MINED THE CHESTATEE RIVER

The Chestatee River cuts through the richest portion of Lumpkin County's gold belt and acts like a natural sluice. While the average miner was limited to what he could pan by wading in shallow creeks and branches, the more affluent prospectors began to devise ways to retrieve gold accumulated in riverbeds.

The earliest known reference to the use of a boat for mining gold in the Chestatee River was reported in the April 9, 1833 issue of the *Auraria Western Herald*. The newspaper noted, "Mr. McCollum…a gentleman of character for enterprise and mechanical genius, has just constructed in the neighborhood, a boat with a diving bell attached to it for the purpose of raising gravel, and collecting gold from the bed of water courses. The boat was launched in the Chestatee River on Friday evening last in our presence, and we feel confident in saying that we believe the example will be followed by many."

The following item was reported in the November 6, 1875 issue of the *Dahlonega Mountain Signal*:

> *The most curious of all the operations of the mines is the boat enterprise of the Loud, Cook & Co. This is a curiously constructed boat, with very fine machinery, for letting down a very large caisson, or diving bell, 6 by 14 by 8 feet high. When lowered to the river bed, air is pumped in and the water excluded, the miners working dry shoal on the bottom of the river. The operation, in our opinion, will be a perfect success, and barrels of gold will be taken from the riverbed by this novel method.*

It wasn't until the latter part of the nineteenth century that dredge mining was done on a large scale. In 1896 State Geologist W.S. Yeates reported that "six or eight boats" had been dredging the bottom of the Chestatee and washing the dredgings for gold "with varying results."

Dredge boats were built in a large excavation pit dug a short distance from the river. When the dredge was completed, a wide canal running between the river and the pit was flooded, allowing the boat to float through the ditch into the river. The earliest dredge boats were pulled upriver by teams of horses. Later, operators burned wood stacked along the riverbank to steam power the dredges. Most of the dredge boats scooped sand and gravel from the riverbed with dippers or buckets attached to a moving belt. Digging deep into the river, the dippers dumped the ore inside the hull of the boat, where miners washed it and captured the gold with mercury placed on the floor of the vessel.

Compared to the relatively small size of the Chestatee River, some of the later dredge boats were huge, measuring ninety feet long and thirty feet wide, with two-foot by two-foot end beams obviously cut from enormous trees. The *Dahlonega Nugget* printed the following description of the *Seawell*: "An up to date very large boat, far greater than any that has ever been built in this country. It will have 71 dippers, each weighing 500 pounds…Some of the natives say that the boat will be too large to float, which tickles those who have seen still larger ones of the kind built and in operation."

Some dredges met with disasters. The Loud, Cook & Company boat and diving bell was sunk, reportedly due to sabotage while tied to the bank. The dredge, operated by Messrs. Birch and Ammons of Kansas City, Missouri, was swept away from its moorings by a freshet (flash flood) and collided with an iron bridge. It was, however, repaired and put back into service. The *Dahlonega Nugget* gave the following report about another ill-fated dredge: "They have had a lot of trouble down at the Seawell boat...The dam bursted letting the vessel down on the bottom, and after working some time in getting it in position again, it was found that a big two-inch rod had broke right square in two on account of the strain being so great."

Freshets that turned the Chestatee into a raging torrent were a real concern for dredge boats. On January 3, 1902, the *Dahlonega Nugget* reported, "Sunday morning when the distress whistle was sounded on the Birch or Breyman boat everyone who heard it knew that the Chestatee river was dangerously high for this whistle makes no false reports."

If heavy rains posed danger for the dredges, lack of rain could bring their work to a standstill by lowering the level of the river until they were left high and dry. "In August of 1902, the Hager dredge was reported "hung up on rock at New Bridge unable to move until the water rises." If a drought was not too severe, a dredge could use its buckets to pile up mud and rock, damming the river to create a pool deep enough to keep it afloat.

Cold weather also posed problems. On February 23, 1900, the *Nugget* reported, "The Birch boat in the Chestatee was not able to operate during the cold wave that visited this whole up country last Saturday and the machinery ceased moving until Monday at noon."

This dredge boat operated on the Chestatee River circa 1912, dredging up gold-bearing mud from the river bottom. *Courtesy of the Georgia Department of Archives and History.*

While earlier dredges were steam driven, turn-of-the-century dredge boats were operated and illumined by electricity, enabling them to work at night. Electricity was used for gold mining in Lumpkin County as early as 1886. It was generated by water-powered wheels at dam sites along the river and extended to the dredge boats by long power lines.

Floods and droughts, difficulty in getting easements, equipment failure and vandalism all contributed to the demise of the great dredge boats. The foreclosure of the *Seawell* dredge was announced in the June 27, 1917 issue of the *Dahlonega Nugget*.

George Loggins may have been the last person who worked on one of the old dredge boats. He was eighty-seven when he was interviewed in 1991, and he still had vivid memories of washing the dredgings and dumping carts of sandy gravel back into the river. He attributed the demise of the dredges to the rising costs of getting easements. "We were getting a right smart of gold but not enough to make a profit," he explained.

## FAMOUS EARLY MINES

### *The Calhoun Mine*

The land along the Chestatee River where Benjamin Parks claimed to have discovered gold in 1828 was purchased for $6,000 in June of 1833. The buyer was John C. Calhoun, the former U.S. vice president who had been elected U.S. senator from South Carolina the previous year.

A few months earlier the current owner of the property had discovered a lump of gold ore weighing over nine pounds. The *Auraria Western Herald* described the rock as containing "one hundred and twenty-four particles of gold upon its surface, plainly perceptible to the eye." This astonishing find may well have influenced Calhoun to purchase the property.

Calhoun employed twenty hands to work what came to be known as the Calhoun Mine. In a letter written to a relative in 1833, Calhoun related that mining activities in Lumpkin County were "universally doing well," and he noted, "I could not hear of an instance of unsuccessful operation…and some were doing most extraordinary business."

Calhoun was in Washington in May of 1842 when a "fabulously rich vein" was discovered at his mine near Dahlonega. Since the senator's political duties prevented him from leaving the Capitol, he turned the mine over to his son-in-law, Thomas G. Clemson, who was a mining engineer. Clemson wrote a friend, "I have often taken from two to five hundred dollars from a single pan of ore." He considered the mine to be "among the richest gold mines ever discovered." In later years he reportedly used some of the wealth from the celebrated Calhoun Mine to found Clemson Agricultural College (now Clemson University) in South Carolina.

After Clemson left the area, the Calhoun Mine was worked intermittently until 1879, when it was purchased from one of Calhoun's heirs by J.A. Bostwick from New York. Bostwick invested heavily in a large operation that included a forty-stamp gold mill and other mining machinery. The mine's superintendent was from New York, but the assistant superintendent was Andrew Jackson Reese of Dahlonega.

The mine was in operation only about a year when both the superintendent and assistant superintendent died. Subsequently, Bostwick donated the property to North Georgia

This photo shows the log-crib dam and a portion of the stamp mill at the Calhoun Mine, Dahlonega's oldest and most famous gold mine. *Courtesy of the Georgia Department of Archives and History.*

Agricultural College with the sole condition that the gift should remain anonymous until after his death.

NGAC trustees leased the mine to W.R. Crisson, who paid the college royalties from the gold he recovered from the property. The operation came to a halt when a disastrous flood washed away a large portion of the dam. As the college had no funds to rebuild it, the mine and mill remained idle until the property was sold in 1889. A portion of the money from the sale was used to erect a two-story brick building named Bostwick Hall in honor of the school's generous benefactor, J.A. Bostwick. The building burned in 1912.

## *The "Free Jim" Mine*

James Bosclair, who was known as "Free Jim," came to Dahlonega from Augusta at the height of the gold rush. He opened a cake and fruit shop and operated an icehouse where he stored natural ice during the winter months to sell the following summer.

When Bosclair could get away from his business, he took a gold pan and went prospecting. He hit pay dirt when he uncovered a rich vein of gold ore on lot 998, east of town, but he couldn't purchase the property because as a "free person of color," he was forbidden by Georgia law to buy or sell real estate. He explained his situation to Dr. Joseph J. Singleton, superintendent of the Dahlonega Mint, who agreed to serve as Bosclair's legal guardian and purchase the property for him.

Bosclair worked the Free Jim Mine successfully for a decade, making enough money in the process to establish a large general merchandise store in Dahlonega. He also ran a popular saloon and was once indicted for selling whiskey on Sunday. He was expelled from the Dahlonega Baptist Church for "selling goods and liquor on Sunday," but he was readmitted a year or so later "on recantation." He was not allowed to obtain a liquor license but solved the problem by putting a white person in charge of the bar of his saloon.

When gold was discovered in California, Bosclair was wealthy enough to grubstake (outfit) nearly fifty men in exchange for half their first year's earnings. Instead of increasing his wealth, however, his trip to California cost him his life when he was shot to death by a disgruntled miner in a dispute over a claim.

## *The Battle Branch Mine*

The name of this mine grew out of an incident that took place very early in the gold rush. Although many miners in the area were from other states, this particular mine was worked by a group of Georgians. When some traders from Tennessee came to the mining camp to sell pork and other food items, they watched the miners plucking shiny gold nuggets out of their pans and soon decided they could get richer by panning than by being sutlers. The Georgia miners, however, didn't take kindly to having competition, and the outcome was a lively brawl with shovels and rocks wielded as weapons. One man was killed and a number of others were wounded, but when the fray was over the Georgians still stood their ground. Nobody knows what the mine was called prior to that time, but it has been called the Battle Branch Mine since that day.

In 1843 an Englishman named Major John Hockenhull began working the mine with a dozen men. After two months of hard work, the only result was a huge open cut. By this time Major Hockenhull's resources and credit were all but exhausted and his laborers were grumbling about not getting paid. When Hockenhull explained his situation, only John Pasco thought it worthwhile to continue working for him. Legend says that when the two men resumed their work later that day, they soon struck a pocket of gold with nuggets ranging in size from a pea to an acorn. Hockenhull reportedly took $80,000 worth of gold from the Battle Branch before retiring from mining.

## *The Petticoat Mine*

Dahlonega's July 3, 1875 *Mountain Signal* reported the following story about how this early mine got its name. One day when a group of men were mining a particularly rich stream, a number of women appeared, filled their petticoats with rocks and began pelting the men with them. The women eventually drove the miners away and took possession of their "diggins" on what came to be called the Petticoat Mine on Petticoat Branch.

## *The Findley Chute*

Shortly after James Jefferson Findley purchased property on Crown Mountain in 1858, he hired Charles Duncan to prospect his new lot for gold. Duncan was reputed to be one of the best prospectors in the area. He claimed to be part Indian and said that he could dream where to find gold.

Whether Duncan had a prophetic dream or a sixth sense about gold or he was just lucky, he soon located a small but remarkably rich vein which became famous in the annals of Lumpkin County gold mining history as the Findley Chute.

Findley and his partner excavated an inclined shaft "sufficiently large to permit three men to work at the same time." The rich yields from the mine were reportedly carried to the Dahlonega Mint in a bucket after dark to avoid attracting attention. However, operations came to an abrupt halt after several months when water filled the shaft to a depth of eight to ten feet.

In 1878 the Findley Gold Mining Company of New York City purchased the property for $30,000. The company's prospectus noted that the Findley lot "is conceded by everyone to contain the largest mass of gold-bearing ores in the Southern belt." Findley Ridge, called the "backbone" of the Georgia gold belt by mining engineers and geologists, was described as "a precipitous ridge, jutting into the valley, with almost sheer ascent of 500 feet above the level of the river."

The prospectus described the celebrated Findley Chute as "a clear, lively quartz lode about three feet thick, carrying a remarkably rich 'pay streak' of two to eight inches, and yielding in many places almost pure masses of gold." Despite the glowing description of the Findley property and its potential, the Findley Gold Mining Company did not prosper. The superintendent, a young man just out of mining school, was unwilling to listen to experienced local miners. He was unable to locate the renowned vein, and after some work in the open cuts, the operation was terminated.

In 1880 a local miner named R.B. King leased the property and located the missing Findley Chute almost immediately. He mined it with great success, but just before his year's lease expired, he "lost" it intentionally so he wouldn't have to reveal its whereabouts! He reportedly made enough from the vein in twelve months to start a bank in Denver, Colorado.

An article entitled "Excitement Over the Rediscovery of a Long Lost Mine" and featuring "Dahlonega, the Center of Yellow Metal Enterprises" was published in the *Atlanta Journal* in 1901. The writer described how two miners, determined to locate the "long-lost treasure," had blasted their way into a tunnel where they saw "an almost solid mass of gold nuggets sticking out like warts on the face of the quartz." "The seams in the rock are full of nuggets," the *Journal* correspondent wrote, "and in many cases the quartz is held together with pure gold." Mining operations at the Findley Mine continued off and on until World War II put a halt to mining.

2

# DAHLONEGA: SEAT OF GOVERNMENT FOR LUMPKIN COUNTY

## THE LAND LOTTERY OF 1832

The state of Georgia held five lotteries between 1805 and 1827 to parcel out Indian lands obtained by treaties. George Gilmer, who was governor when gold was discovered in north Georgia, was not in favor of another lottery, believing it would be more advantageous for the state to maintain control of the mines. He pointed out that state operation of the gold mines would lower taxes and provide revenue needed to improve roads and public education.

The lottery issue was hotly debated in the gubernatorial campaign of 1831. Gilmer's opponent, Wilson Lumpkin, was an enthusiastic supporter of the lottery. In the end the lure of Cherokee land and gold proved to be irresistible to the majority of Georgians. Soon after they voted for Wilson Lumpkin and the lottery, teams of surveyors were tramping through the hills of north Georgia partitioning the Cherokee lands. Most districts were divided into 160-acre lots, but the thirty-three gold districts were divided into 40-acre lots.

The statewide lottery was scheduled to begin in October of 1832. In December the Georgia Legislature divided the region previously designated Cherokee County into ten smaller counties, including Lumpkin County, named for Governor Wilson Lumpkin.

Everyone expected the mining boomtown called Auraria to become the county seat of government for Lumpkin County, as it was the only real settlement in the area. As it turned out, a "fraudulent draw" in the lottery necessitated a change of plans. The man who drew the Auraria land lot had claimed to be head of a household, which entitled him to two draws. When he was discovered to be a bachelor, the legalities of the case made it likely to be tied up in court for months. Since a seat of government was needed immediately, the Inferior Court began looking for another suitable lot where they could acquire a clear title and build a courthouse without delay. The site selected for the Public Square and courthouse was a little over five miles north of Auraria. As someone quipped, that was the only piece of ground that was level enough!

## THE NAMING OF DAHLONEGA

If Dahlonega had been named for a founding father like so many other towns in Georgia, it might well have been called "Parksville" in honor of Benjamin Parks, who is credited with being the first person to discover gold in the area. Parks was indirectly responsible for the village's first unofficial name, Licklog.

According to legend, Parks and a friend who was married to a Cherokee woman were allowed to keep cattle in Indian Territory west of the Chestatee River. They put out salt for their stock in a trough made of a hollowed-out log called a licklog. After Lumpkin County was organized on December 3, 1832, the site selected to be the county seat of government was very near this cattle saltlick. When the first small log courthouse was built in the center of the just-laid-out Public Square, the site had not yet been officially named and was popularly referred to as Licklog. Mail was addressed to "Lumpkin Court House."

The new county seat was also called "New Mexico" in some early court documents. The Macon newspaper, the *Georgia Messenger*, published the following item in the October 17, 1833 issue: "New Mexico, a mining camp, was selected by the inferior court as the county seat of Lumpkin County in 1833, but the name was changed to Talonega, or Dahlonega, the Cherokee word for yellow metal." It has been suggested that Mexican miners who came to the area may have called it "New Mexico," but the origin of the name has been lost over the years.

James Mooney, who is noted for his extensive study of Cherokee words, suggested that the original word was "da-le-ni-gei," meaning "yellow," but it was spelled various ways before being finalized as "Dahlonega." In announcing that the new seat of government had been given its name in October of 1833, Auraria's *Western Herald* used the spelling "Talonega." An act of the Georgia Legislature incorporating the town spelled it "Talonaga."

After an educated Cherokee informed the editor of the *Western Herald* that the correct spelling should be "Dahlohnega," a cumbersome second "h" was adopted and used in legal documents for a short period before being dropped. Writing the unusual name of the new county seat was a challenge, and many simply wrote it the way it sounded to them. Some interesting and creative variations included "Tahlauneca," and "Dablobuega."

## LUMPKIN COUNTY'S 1836 COURTHOUSE

*But above all, the courthouse: the center, the focus, the hub; sitting looming in the center of the county's circumference...musing, brooding, symbolic and ponderable, tall as cloud, solid as rock, dominating all...*
*From* Requiem for a Nun *by William Faulkner*

When surveyors laid out the plat for the village designated as the seat of government for Lumpkin County, a rare area of mostly level ground was selected for the Public Square. It was to be a place where citizens could "assemble peaceably and speak freely, exercising rights guaranteed to them by the Constitution of the United States." A small log building was quickly erected in the center of the Public Square to serve as the county courthouse until a larger and more permanent structure could be built. Crisson family history says that fifteen-year-old W. Reese Crisson helped clear the land and build the log courthouse. In later years he wrote the following description of it: "A temporary courthouse 18 by 32 feet was constructed of split logs and pine poles. The door of the structure was so low that when a tall man undertook to enter the courthouse, it was necessary for him to stoop and go in half bent. If this step was neglected, he was likely to crush his hat or ruffle his precious scalp. The door being only three feet wide, very large men found it convenient to enter the courthouse edgewise by a kind of side-step."

The first session of court convened on August 22, 1833, eight months after the county was organized by an act of the Georgia legislature. The crowd gathered around the log courthouse was made up mostly of bearded miners, but a few Cherokees watched curiously from the background.

Those required to be inside the small structure were soon perspiring heavily that August day. They included His Honor, Judge John W. Hooper, who took the judge's seat and rapped his gavel for order. Sheriff Samuel Jones then cried out, "Oh yez, oh yez, the Superior Court of Lumpkin County is now open." The expression "oh yez," taken from the French word "oyez" and meaning "Hear ye," was traditionally used to command silence.

The grand jury's first true bill was found against Jesse N. Brown for the murder of Robert Ligon, postmaster of Auraria. Several men from Auraria were indicted for operating illegal gambling tables for a game known as "chuckaluck." The presentments of that first grand jury included a recommendation to build a new jail and courthouse as soon as possible.

A contract to build a brick courthouse was awarded to John Humphries, who stated in writing that he would "commence next week and complete it in eighteen months" for the sum of $7,000. Unfortunately, Humphries turned out to be a scoundrel. Despite his advance of $2,500 for materials, he had yet to begin work more than a year later. When Deputy Sheriff John D. Fields attempted to serve a warrant on the errant contractor, the man drew a gun and fled. By the time Fields could get a posse together, Humphries had fled the county. His bondsmen were required to repay the money advanced plus interest and the cost of bringing them to court.

A second contract resulted in the erection of a fine two-story brick courthouse in the year1836 by Ephraim Clayton of North Carolina. Clayton's design was a vernacular interpretation of Federal style in the main block and Greek Revival style in the two-story portico. Clayton's son Thomas came to Dahlonega by horse and buggy to receive the final payment due his father, which was paid to him in gold bullion.

Tradition says that the bricks were molded on Brickyard Hill just south of town. They have been found to contain small traces of gold, tending to confirm that they were made locally. Stone for the foundation and timber used in the construction came from the surrounding countryside, as did sand used for mortar, but the hardware had to be imported from Augusta.

## "THERE'S MILLIONS IN IT!"

When gold was discovered in California in 1848, many local miners—discouraged with the diminished amount of color showing up in their gold pans—determined to pull up stakes

The 1836 Lumpkin County Courthouse is shown here circa 1929 before the Public Square was paved. It is Georgia's oldest surviving courthouse. *Courtesy of the Georgia Department of Archives and History.*

and seek their fortunes in the new gold fields. Dr. Matthew F. Stephenson, a man of science actively involved in numerous local mining operations, was convinced that there was still an abundance of gold in Lumpkin County that could be recovered using scientific methods.

On a day when the Public Square was full of departing miners, Dr. Stephenson climbed the steps to the second-story porch of the courthouse in order to address them, using all his oratorical skills to dissuade them from leaving. Gesturing dramatically southward toward Findley Ridge, the mother lode from which gold had eroded into the rivers and streams below, he cried, "Boys, there's millions in it!"

Despite Stephenson's eloquent efforts, many miners set out on the long and dangerous journey to California. Even though they didn't take his advice, they remembered his words and frequently used them as a general expression of enthusiasm and encouragement.

"There's millions in it!" became such a popular saying in the West that American humorist and writer Samuel Clemens, more commonly known as Mark Twain, quoted it in his book *The Gilded Age*. Following the publication of Twain's book, Stephenson's now-famous words were quoted all over the English-speaking world. However, few people know that they originated in the little mining village of Dahlonega in the mountains of north Georgia.

## UNUSUAL USES OF THE COURTHOUSE

If the courthouse could talk, what tales it could tell! On one occasion when the jury was deliberating, one of the jurors dropped a string from a second-story window down to an accomplice, who tied it to a jug of "spirituous liquor." It is not known how much of the whiskey was imbibed before it was detected and confiscated.

In 1854 Jesse Henley was shoved down the stairs, causing him to fall against a sharp corner and suffer internal injuries. The victim was carried into the courtroom, where three doctors attended him before he expired seven days later.

The courthouse was again used as a hospital some years later when Dr. E.F. Starr performed surgery on Ben Satterfield to remove a kidney stone. A century later, Sheriff Jack Gillespie was murdered just outside the courthouse on election night. On another occasion the building was the scene of a funeral service when a man about to be hanged as a horse thief wanted to hear his funeral before he died. His wish was granted.

## THE COURTHOUSE DURING THE CIVIL WAR

Although there were few slaveholders in Lumpkin County, black slaves were occasionally bought and sold in front of the courthouse. After the onset of the Civil War, local volunteer units such as the Blue Ridge Rifles mustered in front of the courthouse where they were presented with Confederate flags and sent off with heartfelt patriotic encouragement. At such times the courthouse was the scene of many impassioned speeches.

In 1863 the grand jury recommended that the courthouse be turned over to the military. The building was utilized as a headquarters and military prison during the remainder of the war. Most of those imprisoned there were deserters and mountain men who refused to fight for the Confederacy because of Union sympathies.

## "TEMPLE OF JUSTICE" IN NEED OF REPAIRS

In 1879 *Harper's New Monthly Magazine* published an article about gold mining in Lumpkin County that included a description and drawing of the courthouse. The village of Dahlonega was described as clustered around its "once imposing but now half-ruined courthouse," which may have been a contributing factor to the repairs made to the building later that year.

Articles in the January 1880 *Dahlonega Mountain Signal* related how the "Temple of Justice" had been remodeled, making it "as good as new and decidedly prettier." Noting previous abuse by "the ill bred idly whittling on the railing, etc.," Editor Howell recommended a law "against the commission of public indecencies on the premises."

The courthouse seems to have been perennially in need of repairs. Some years later, Editor W.B. Townsend lamented the condition of the structure with these words published in the *Dahlonega Nugget*: "Our court house looks more like an old barn than a place for the dishing out of justice. Some of the blinds are gone, down spout broke loose, sixteen window panes out and no latch on the front door. The Court and jury had better bring their overcoats and a foot stove to keep them comfortable in case a cold spell was to come at court week."

In 1899 the brick floors on the ground level were either removed or covered with concrete because pigs wandering loose around town made their way through the open doors into the courthouse and rooted up the bricks. The four corner rooms were built by private individuals with the county's permission and housed various establishments, including an eatery and a doctor's office. The center portion of the ground floor was an open market.

## *LIFE* MAGAZINE FEATURES COURT WEEK IN DAHLONEGA

Court week was a big event in Dahlonega, and people from out in the county flocked to town to watch the trials and socialize. While court was in recess, folks gathered to watch shows put on by the medicine man and listen to him hawk his wares.

The September 21, 1942 issue of *Life* magazine featured a seven-page article about court week in Dahlonega. The numerous pictures included provide a valuable record of the interior and exterior appearance of the courthouse as well as the personalities, automobiles and dress of the day.

Moonshiners in overalls are shown pleading guilty for making liquor illegally and receiving fines of $75 apiece. A woman in a flowered dress, her head lowered in shame, was charged with violating the state's then strict laws on morality and was sentenced to pay a $42.85 fine or serve twelve months in jail. She chose to pay the fine. Sheriff Joe Davis was photographed standing beside the bench wearing his hat, which he—unlike other men in the courtroom—did not remove, in accordance with an old English (rather than the American) court custom.

## FROM COURTHOUSE TO GOLD MUSEUM

As Dahlonega and Lumpkin County grew over the years, the old courthouse was no longer adequate in size. In 1965 a new courthouse was built several blocks east of the Public Square. For a time, the fate of the historic structure hung in the balance when some of the local merchants wanted it torn down to make more room for parking on the square.

Meetings were held at the courthouse to discuss whether the building could be preserved as a museum. Most local citizens favored preservation but didn't know how it could be financed. A committee was formed to ask Governor Carl Sanders for assistance from his contingency fund. The Georgia Historical Commission voted to supervise the project, which involved intensive repairs both inside and out.

As renovation began, architect Garland Reynolds feared the ancient building would collapse before he could get it stabilized. "When we took the plaster off the inside walls... the mud mortar under the plaster had become dust," he was quoted as saying in the June 4, 1967 *Atlanta Journal and Constitution* magazine. "I had plasterers come in quick and put on a scratch coat of new plaster in a hurry to keep the old plaster in place. On the outside, we sandblasted to restore the original brick color, scratched out the mud, replaced it with mortar and then sealed the exterior with silicone waterproofing."

The original ground-floor lobby, which had disappeared in an accumulation of partitioned offices and restrooms, was reclaimed from the architectural jungle. In the days before latrines were added, it was customary for the bailiff to march the jury to a nearby barn to relieve themselves. The county was forced to provide facilities when people began keeping their barns locked during court week!

In the process of removing partitions, workers discovered one of the original nine-foot Doric columns supporting the upstairs courtroom floor. The other was missing but was later found nine miles from town in use as an outdoor light pole. While repairing numerous woodpecker holes in the column, workmen discovered a bullet hole. Bullets were also found embedded in the elm trees growing next to the building.

Much of the credit for saving the old courthouse goes to a local woman named Madeleine Anthony, who was one of the first to recognize the importance of preserving local history. She never had to lie down in front of bulldozers, but the feisty Madeleine would not have hesitated to do so had it been necessary to save her beloved courthouse. She retrieved boxes of discarded records that had been consigned to the landfill.

Madeleine also rescued discarded bricks from the floor, which were later sold to raise funds for the new library. Each brick came with a brass plaque inscribed "Lumpkin County Courthouse 1836" and a copy of an assay report showing traces of gold. When the old courthouse reopened its doors as the Dahlonega Gold Museum on July 1, 1967, Madeleine Anthony was its able curator who fascinated visitors with her knowledge and enthusiasm about local history.

Curator Anthony kept a U.S. map and asked people visiting the Gold Museum to color in the state they were from. Her goal was to record visitors from every state in the Union, but nobody had come from faraway Alaska. Undaunted, the curator called the local sheriff and explained what she needed. A few days later, a car with an Alaska license plate passing through town was pulled over by an official vehicle with flashing lights. The bewildered driver was informed that he was free to go—as soon as he visited the Gold Museum and colored in the state of Alaska!

Today the Dahlonega Gold Museum is operated by the Georgia Department of Natural Resources. It is visited annually by 62,000 people from all over the world. The museum offers written information in seven different languages, and videos in Spanish, German and Italian as well as English. Approximately 6,000 students make field trips to tour the museum annually.

A display case downstairs contains numerous gold nuggets along with a complete collection of rare gold coins made at the Dahlonega Branch Mint. An overhead video tells the story of the mint and gold mining in north Georgia and shows enlarged pictures of the coins.

The mining room uses extensive photographs and displays to demonstrate how gold was extracted and processed, while the mint room tells the story of the United States Mint that operated in Dahlonega from 1838 until the beginning of the Civil War in 1861. On display are the original weights and measures used at the mint and the only known photograph of the old building. Upstairs in the original courtroom, visitors view a film in which the last of the old-time miners give colorful descriptions of their personal mining experiences.

The Dahlonega Gold Museum is located in Georgia's oldest surviving courthouse and the oldest public building in north Georgia. It is open from 9:00 a.m. to 5:00 p.m. seven days a week except for Christmas, New Year's and Thanksgiving. The 1836 Lumpkin County Courthouse is recognized within the Dahlonega Historic Commercial District as listed on the National Register of Historic Places.

## DAHLONEGA'S FIRST CHURCHES

In the early days of Dahlonega, the mining village was a rough and rowdy place. According to an eyewitness account, "Gambling houses, dancing houses, drinking saloons, houses of ill fame, billiard saloons, and tenpin alleys were open day and night." The women were described as "equally as vile and wicked" as the men.

Drunken miners were such a nuisance that the grand jury for the August 1835 term felt "compelled to call the attention of our fellow citizens to the increasing number of tippling shops in our county," which was viewed as having "a most injurious and demoralizing influence upon our community."

Gambling devices reportedly could be seen on the Public Square both day and night and especially on the weekends. Arguments frequently erupted over claims of cheating and quickly turned into free-for-alls that made the night "hideous with fighting, cursing and swearing" in which "hundreds of combatants were sometimes seen at fisticuffs, swearing, striking and gouging."

When the first churches were organized, men and women who wanted Dahlonega to be a decent place to raise their families worked to change the atmosphere of the community. Liquor saloons were closed on Sunday and gambling houses were required to close at midnight. Colonel W.P. Price wrote in 1897 that "numbers of vile, lewd women were removed by men and boys from the town without any authority of law, except public opinion."

### *Dahlonega Baptist Church*

The first Baptists to meet as a church assembled on March 27, 1835, to lay the foundation for the "Baptist Church of Christ, at Kimzey creek." Membership grew from seven to more than fifty over the next three years. In September of 1838, a number of the members "retired to town," as stated in the church minutes, and took the name "Baptist Church of Christ at Dahlonega." They held services in the Dahlonega Academy until they could build a house of worship in 1841. This two-story frame building, located near the U.S. Mint, had a free-standing bell tower instead of a steeple on top.

Prior to the Civil War, blacks and whites attended church together, but the black people also held their own services on Sunday afternoon or evening. The black community organized the First Baptist Church in 1866 and held services in a brush arbor until the congregation could build its own house of worship in 1871. Their first church building was located on a knoll northeast of town called Crane's Hill.

By the 1890s the Dahlonega Baptist Church of Christ had outgrown its 1841 frame building, which was also badly in need of repairs. In 1897 ground was broken on a lot

Dahlonega Baptists built their first church in 1841. The two-story frame structure had a separate bell tower instead of a steeple. *Courtesy of the Georgia Department of Archives and History.*

donated by Colonel W.P. Price for a new brick structure. It is written in the annals of local history that the foundation was "laid of granite fresh from a newly-opened gold mine" and "particles of gold could be seen with the naked eye in some of these rocks." The church's baptistery was lined with copper made from old stills donated by former moonshiners. Colonel Price was not only chairman of the building committee; he also personally contributed a fourth of the $4,200 building cost.

An unexpected problem was encountered when the owner of an adjoining lot began erecting "an unsightly wooden shack which, if completed, would…endanger the Church itself from fire, to say nothing of the ungainly sight of the building thus being erected." The church was forced to purchase the lot—just as the unscrupulous owner had schemed—in order to remove the offending shack.

Civilian construction was at a standstill during World War II, but soon after the armistice, plans were made for expansion. By 1950 the church sanctuary had been enlarged and a new three-story education wing had been added so that the church now stretched all the way across the block from Chestatee Street to Park Street. In 1981 the church purchased the Whitmire house and warehouse next door and combined them into one building to be used for educational and fellowship activities as well as a media center and offices.

The 1897 building with its added education wing served Dahlonega Baptists well for a hundred years. By the turn of the century, however, continued growth necessitated a larger facility. In 2001 they moved into a new building located on a hill overlooking the town. The architecture of the new church was designed to be reminiscent of the beloved old building, with an offset bell tower accentuated on two sides with round windows circling a cross.

## *Dahlonega Methodist Church*

In 1835 "the people called the Methodist church were encouraged and stimulated in their Christian work by the presence of a regular pastor among them." Although the church was not officially organized until the arrival of a pastor, people of the Methodist persuasion were apparently already active in the gold mining village called Dahlonega.

Methodists held services in the Dahlonega Academy until they built this house of worship on Park Street circa 1840. Graves of two Revolutionary War soldiers were covered up when the structure was enlarged in 1853. *Courtesy of the author.*

In 1839 these Methodists purchased land on Park Street, and their first house of worship is believed to have been erected the following year. Prior to that time they held services in the Dahlonega Academy. In 1853 the original thirty-by-forty-foot structure was enlarged by twenty feet to accommodate the increase in membership following "a most remarkable revival."

The old frame building was torn down in 1929 to make way for a new brick structure. Church members excavating the foundation discovered two forgotten graves, which had been covered over when the former structure was enlarged in 1853. It was determined that two Revolutionary War veterans had been buried there. The few remains, including several well-preserved teeth, some locks of hair and a button, were reinterred at Mount Hope Cemetery. A copper receptacle containing church records was deposited in the northwest corner of the foundation of the new building. The copper came from a still destroyed by government agents.

Dahlonega Methodists began their new church building on the eve of the stock market crash that resulted in the Great Depression, and they carried it through to completion in the midst of the resulting economic collapse. The church's beautiful stained glass windows were commissioned by member Will O. Reese, who knew an Atlanta stained glass company willing to make the windows at sacrificial prices in order to get work.

In 1939 the name of Dahlonega Methodist Episcopal Church, South, was changed to Dahlonega Methodist Church. It was changed again in 1968 to become Dahlonega United Methodist Church when the Methodist Church and the Evangelical United Brethren Church merged to become one denomination.

Methodists of today still worship on the same site as Dahlonega's first Methodists. The seventy-six-year-old structure, supplemented by a modern fellowship hall, accommodates the rapidly growing congregation by means of a number of services.

## *Dahlonega Presbyterian Church*

The Presbyterians of Dahlonega were organized in 1838 by their first pastor, Reverend David Hastings Mason, who came from Philadelphia in 1837 to be a coiner at the Dahlonega Branch Mint. Mason was responsible for the construction of a building that served as the Presbyterian place of worship downstairs and a Masonic lodge upstairs.

This building was occupied by a garrison of Federal soldiers during the Civil War and was so badly damaged that it was torn down. The lumber was used to build Wimpy's Mill on Yahoola Creek. During the years when the Presbyterians were without a building of their own, they held services in both the Baptist and Methodist churches.

Although the first Presbyterians were small in number, they were active in the community. Soon after they were organized in 1838, they established a Sunday school in the Dahlonega Academy. Frederick D. Boartfield, who came to Dahlonega from Philadelphia as part of David Mason's workforce at the U.S. Mint, was superintendent of the Union Sunday School for twelve years.

Over the years the Presbyterian Church had close ties with both the Dahlonega Mint and North Georgia Agricultural College. Not only was it established by the mint's chief coiner, but another officer of the mint—Colonel Robert Hughes Moore—also donated the land where the first church was erected.

The earliest Presbyterian church was damaged by occupying troops during the Civil War and torn down. This frame structure was built in 1899. *Courtesy of Jimmy Anderson.*

Dr. B.P. Gaillard, professor at the college for sixty years, and his family were among the church's staunchest supporters from the time they arrived in Dahlonega in 1873. At that time the church was "in a dormant state" with only a few members. Dr. Isaac W. Waddell—president of NGAC from 1893 until 1898—served as pastor of Dahlonega Presbyterian Church.

Many efforts were made over the years to build a church home of their own, but the Presbyterian membership was not strong enough to raise the necessary capital. After thirty years of having to use other facilities, the Presbyterians were finally able to erect a fine frame church building on North Park Street in 1899.

In 1962 the Presbyterians sold their church building to the Archdiocese of Atlanta to become St. Luke's Catholic Church. Shortly afterward the Presbyterians erected a new brick structure west of the Public Square on or very near the site of their original church built by Reverend Mason.

## THE CHEROKEE REMOVAL ON THE TRAIL OF TEARS

By the time the Lumpkin County Courthouse was built in 1836, some Cherokees—seeing that they were powerless to stop the white intruders from taking their land—had voluntarily moved to land given to them in the West. Others trusted that their chief, John Ross, would be able to negotiate a treaty with the Federal government that would allow them to remain in their homes, despite the fact that the state of Georgia had already claimed jurisdiction over their land.

In 1835 a few Cherokee leaders signed a treaty agreeing to surrender all of their land in Georgia for an equivalent amount in the West and five million dollars. Despite bitter protests that these few were not authorized to represent all the Cherokee people, the treaty was enforced by the U.S. Government. It stipulated that any Indians who had not voluntarily moved to the West by May 23, 1838, would be forcibly removed. On that day, soldiers under the command of General Winfield Scott were sent to round up all Cherokees remaining in north Georgia and take them to holding stockades referred to as stations.

Cherokees in Lumpkin County were taken to a station located south of Dahlonega near the mining community of Auraria. From there they walked to Ross's Landing near the Tennessee border to join those brought in from other areas. Approximately twelve thousand Cherokees were divided into thirteen detachments, which left a few days apart beginning September 1. Although some wagons were provided, many walked the entire distance to Oklahoma, some barefooted. The last groups to leave in late November and early December suffered greatly from traveling through snow and ice, and many died on the arduous journey they called "The Trail Where They Cried," the infamous Trail of Tears.

An eyewitness described seeing the Cherokees pass through Kentucky on a freezing December day with these words: "When I passed the last detachment of those suffering exiles and thought my native countrymen had thus expelled them from their native soil and their much-loved homes, and that too in this inclement season of the year in all their suffering, I turned from the sight with feelings which language cannot express."

*3*

# DAHLONEGA: SITE OF A UNITED STATES MINT

## THE NEED FOR MORE COINS IN CIRCULATION

Coins were in very short supply in the early 1800s; thus, miners had to use gold as a medium of exchange for their purchases. In the early days of the Georgia gold rush, the going price for a drink of whiskey was reported to be "the amount of gold dust that would lie on the point of a knife." Before business establishments acquired gold scales to weigh a customer's payment, and even afterward, miners frequently complained that they were not given full value for their raw gold.

The alternative was not any more satisfactory. Although some miners did ship their gold to the United States Mint in Philadelphia to be coined, this process involved long delays and the danger of the shipment being lost or stolen.

In November 1833, a group of miners met at the Paschal Hotel in Auraria to discuss the need for a nearby mint to put local gold into coins of clearly defined values. John C. Calhoun, the senator from South Carolina who owned profitable mining property in Lumpkin County, was a strong proponent of the idea.

## THE MINT ACT OF 1835

When a bill was introduced in Congress in 1834 calling for branch mints to be established in the vicinity of the Southern mines, a group of local citizens wrote to Senator Calhoun, urging that one of the proposed mints be erected in Lumpkin County. They pointed out that it was centrally located in the gold region and was "most contiguous to the principal mining operations & to the Chestatee River, which is known of itself to be the richest of all the mines..."

The Mint Bill sparked hot debate in the Senate, but Senator Calhoun's strong support helped to ensure its passage by a margin of twenty-four to nineteen. The Mint Act of 1835 called for the establishment of three branch mints: one in New Orleans to coin gold and silver; one in Charlotte, North Carolina, to coin gold; and a branch "at or near Dahlonega, in Lumpkin County, in the state of Georgia, for the coinage of gold only."

Ignatius Few was appointed commissioner in charge of purchasing land "at or near Dahlonega" on which to build the projected mint. After some searching, he selected a tract of land just south of Dahlonega belonging to William Worley. Few noted that the virgin timber on the ten-acre plot would provide adequate fuel for the mint's operation and that the building site commanded a fine view of the town and surrounding countryside.

While Few was searching for property, local miners were frustrated that it had taken five months from the time Congress passed the bill authorizing the Dahlonega Mint until a building site was purchased. They held a town meeting to draft resolutions, which they sent to President Andrew Jackson and Dr. Robert Patterson, director of the Philadelphia Mint, complaining bitterly about the "unconscionable delay." The irate miners pointed out that the two other branch mints being erected at Charlotte and New Orleans were already "under contract and in a fair way to their completion."

It was decided that the Dahlonega Mint would be erected according to the same plans and budget as the Charlotte Mint, and a contract was awarded to Benjamin Towns, who agreed to do the work for $33,450. Work proceeded slowly due to the difficulty in getting materials and skilled workmen to the remote frontier area.

Machinery for the Dahlonega Mint was shipped from Philadelphia to Savannah on the brig *New Hanover* in April of 1837. From there the boxes were conveyed upriver to Augusta, where they were loaded on ten wagons for the overland trip to the north Georgia mountains—a journey requiring ten to fifteen days, depending upon the weather and condition of the roads.

The Dahlonega Branch Mint officially opened on February 12, 1838, to accept gold bullion deposits. Two months later the mint produced its first coins: eighty $5 gold pieces called "half eagles." Dr. Joseph J. Singleton, the mint's first superintendent, sent a sample to Director Patterson of the Philadelphia Mint along with a letter saying, "You may possibly consider it presumptuous in me to say that I believe our coin equal to any made in the world both for its beauty and accuracy in its legal parts." Ironically, the coins were considered too valuable to be circulated locally!

## EFFECTS OF THE CALIFORNIA GOLD RUSH

After two decades of being steadily mined, the streams and branches in north Georgia had been nearly depleted of their rich gold deposits. As the amount of gold mined in north Georgia dwindled during the 1840s, there was talk of closing the U.S. Mint at Dahlonega, as it was doing little to alleviate the national shortage of currency.

When gold was discovered in California in 1848, many local miners were lured to the rich new gold fields, further depleting the amount of bullion brought to the Dahlonega Mint. By 1850, however, many miners were returning from the West, bringing California gold with them and making the next few years the most prosperous in the history of the mint. In 1851 the amount of California gold deposited at the Dahlonega Mint surpassed the quantity of Georgia gold.

The imported gold affected the color and composition of the coins struck at the Dahlonega Mint. Whereas Georgia gold has very little silver in it (generally no more than 5 percent), California gold contains an average of 15 percent silver.

The U.S. Mint in Dahlonega coined more than $6 million in gold coins during its years of operation, 1838–1861. *Print from the Commissioner of Agriculture Report for 1872.*

According to a little-known but well-documented story, local miners got a head start on other forty-niners as the result of a letter sent from California to mining friends back in Lumpkin County before newspapers began publishing the information.

## JENNIE WIMMER KNEW GOLD WHEN SHE SAW IT

Jennie Cloud came to the Dahlonega gold rush with her family in 1838 when she was sixteen. She and her mother ran a boardinghouse while her father and brother mined for gold, but she liked to try her hand at panning when she had free time. Two years later Jennie and her husband Obadiah immigrated to Missouri to farm. Following his death, she married Peter Wimmer, a widower with five children, and the blended family joined a wagon train to California, where they went to work for Captain Sutter.

Peter was made assistant foreman to James Marshall at Sutter's sawmill on the American River, and Jennie was employed as camp cook and laundress for the crew of workers. When a gold nugget was found in the millrace, Marshall thought it was probably only "fool's gold."

"Let's show it to my wife Jennie," Peter suggested. "She was in the Georgia gold rush and will know if this is real gold or not."

"Why, of course that's gold!" Jennie informed them after a brief glance. When the men doubted her wisdom, she snatched the nugget and dropped it into the boiling pot where she was making soap. "If it's real gold, the lye won't hurt it," she assured them. Sure enough, the next morning when the thick liquid had solidified and the pot was turned upside down to dump out the soap, there was the nugget, looking none the worse after its immersion in the caustic lye solution.

The structure shown is a reconstruction of Sutter's Mill on the American River in Coloma, California, as it appeared when the first gold nugget was found in the millrace in 1848. *Courtesy of the author.*

Despite Captain Sutter's efforts to keep the discovery quiet, word quickly spread in the surrounding area. Stores and other places of business as far away as San Francisco were shut down because the men who ran them had taken to the hills in search of gold. Jennie wasted no time composing a letter to mining friends back in Georgia, telling them about the discovery. Thanks to this advance notice, many Lumpkin County miners were very successful mining for gold in California.

The recipient of Jennie's letter remains a matter of speculation, but the most likely candidate is William Greenberry Russell. "Green" Russell had been mining since he was a young boy and had supported his mother and five siblings with his findings ever since his father's premature death in 1835. The diminishing amount of gold in north Georgia had made the task increasingly difficult, so when news came of a new and more plentiful supply, Green organized a party of miners, including his brother John, to go to California. Their early arrival as well as their previous mining experience gave them a huge advantage over most of the forty-niners, who poured into the California gold fields with little else but high hopes.

By the end of the year Green and John Russell had been so successful that they were ready to head back to Georgia. One of the first things they did upon returning to Lumpkin County was to take their gold to the Dahlonega Mint to be coined. John used his newfound wealth to establish a mercantile business, but Green was home only a few months before heading back to California. Once again he was accompanied by a party of miners, which this time

Jennie Wimmer learned to pan gold in the Georgia gold rush and proved that the shining nugget found at Sutter's Mill was real gold by testing it in her soap pot. *Courtesy of Bert Hughes, a descendant of Jennie Wimmer.*

included his two younger brothers, Joseph Oliver and Levi. Their ship, the SS *Oregon*, reached San Francisco in October 1850, carrying the news of California's admittance into the Union as the thirty-first state.

When the brothers returned to Lumpkin County two years later, Levi was able to fulfill his dream of attending medical school and becoming a doctor. Green used his gold to purchase a five-hundred-acre tract of land on the Etowah River called Savannah Plantation.

## LOCAL MINERS STARTED THE COLORADO GOLD RUSH

Green Russell and his family lived comfortably on the wealth he had mined in the California gold rush until the Financial Panic of 1857, which led to a severe economic depression throughout the United States. Green and his brothers needed a source of income, but by this time gold was as hard to find in California as in Georgia.

Green remembered how he had tested the ore in streams flowing out of the Rocky Mountains on his first trip to California. True, he had found only small amounts of color in his pan, but he knew that placer deposits of gold in Georgia had eroded from veins located in the mountains above the streams. Green wondered if there might not be rich lodes of gold to be found in the Rockies.

In February 1858, Green and his brothers Oliver and Levi, accompanied by a number of other local miners, set out on a nearly two-thousand-mile journey to western Kansas Territory, commonly known as Pike's Peak country. As they approached the Rockies, the Georgia men stared in awe at the rugged snowcapped peaks, which stood in dramatic contrast with the rounded blue-green mountains of north Georgia.

The men paused often along the way to test ore from the streams, but the amount of color they found in their pans was very discouraging. In late June a member of the party named Luke Tierney made the following entry in his journal: "On the twenty-sixth, most of the men spent the day prospecting. On their return to camp, their spirits were very much depressed...The prospect was so far short of their expectations and feverish hopes, that many began to show signs of mortification. They no doubt expected to find lumps of gold like hailstones, all over the surface."

Tierney reported that most of the men in the party abandoned their efforts and went home. Green Russell, however, was not yet ready to give up. "Gentlemen, you can all go, but I'm going to stay if at least two of you will remain with me," he told them.

Twelve men remained with Green, including his loyal brothers, Oliver and Levi. They built a cabin at a location on Cherry Creek and named their camp "Auraria" after the first gold-mining boomtown back home in Lumpkin County.

After many months of largely unproductive panning, a Georgia miner named John H. Gregory uncovered a rich outcropping of gold-bearing quartz in the mountains west of Auraria. This was the first lode or vein gold found anywhere in the area and the news spread rapidly. This area, called Gregory Gulch, was soon overrun with eager prospectors staking their claims.

At the time of Gregory's big strike, Green was on his way back from Georgia with a new mining party of one hundred and seventy hopeful prospectors. When he reached Auraria

Green Russell mined successfully in the nation's first three major gold rushes and was noted for wearing his beard plaited into two braids. This drawing of how he might have looked was done by Dahlonega artist Bill Lawson.

and heard the news, he wasted no time heading into the mountains near Gregory Gulch. In another gulch about three miles south of Gregory's claim, Green had his men spread out in all directions testing for gold. They soon uncovered a productive vein that gave further impetus to the Pike's Peak gold rush.

By the end of September more than eight hundred men were at work in Russell Gulch, which proved to be one of the richest gold-bearing districts in the territory that would become the state of Colorado in 1876. Auraria, the Russells's mining camp on Cherry Creek, was eventually absorbed into another mining camp on the other side of the creek, named Denver City for the governor of Kansas Territory, James W. Denver.

The Russell brothers from Lumpkin County, Georgia, had now mined successfully in the nation's first three major gold rushes and were largely responsible for starting the one in Colorado.

## THE WINDS OF WAR

During the tense months leading up to the outbreak of the Civil War, arguments and fights were common in the Pike's Peak mining camps. The newly created Colorado Territory pledged its allegiance to the Union in September of 1861, and Union sympathizers frequently harassed the Southern miners.

The Russells decided it was time to pull up stakes and head for home, but they had not gotten far when they were arrested and held as political prisoners at Fort Union in New Mexico. In a letter sent to Washington from Santa Fe inquiring what to do about the captured Southerners, General James H. Carlton noted, "The party had some twenty-eight thousand dollars in gold dust which I had deposited in the U.S. Depository in this City." The prisoners were finally told they would be released and all of their property restored to them if they took the oath of allegiance to the United States. Otherwise they would be held until the end of the war. The Russells took the oath and were released on February 14, 1863, but getting home to Georgia involved traveling through enemy territory, where miners with Southern accents were certain to be suspect.

Since travel by daylight was dangerous, the brothers hid in caves or underbrush until nightfall. They dared not build a fire to cook food and were frequently so hungry they chewed slippery elm bark. Their gold was concealed in bags partially filled with horseshoes, which were slung across their saddles so as to be concealed by the riders when mounted.

When the Russell brothers finally arrived home safely, they were warmly greeted by their families, but there was no place to take their fortune in gold to be coined. The Dahlonega Branch Mint had been closed by the Confederate government soon after the beginning of the war.

## THE CLOSING OF THE DAHLONEGA MINT

The Dahlonega Branch Mint continued to operate as usual for four months after Georgia seceded from the Union on January 19, 1861. However, the Georgia Secession Convention claimed jurisdiction over all U.S. Government property in the state, and the Confederate Congress voted to close both the Dahlonega and the New Orleans Mints shortly after hostilities broke out at Fort Sumter in April.

George Kellogg, last superintendent of the Dahlonega Mint, was responsible for closing down operations and shipping all coins and bullion (approximately $25,000 worth) to Charleston for use by the Confederacy. In response to the appeals of local miners, the Confederacy appointed Lewis W. Quillian to maintain an assay office in the mint building. However, there was little gold for him to analyze as mining had come to a standstill with more and more able-bodied men going off to fight. The only time Quillian was busy was in the summer of 1862 when the Confederate government deposited eighteen hundred pounds of gold and silver bullion to be cast into ingots.

Federal troops were sent to Dahlonega and quartered in the mint building for four years following the cessation of hostilities between North and South. A basement room was converted into a prison. After the last soldiers departed in 1869, an inspector from the Philadelphia Mint was sent to Dahlonega to assess the condition of its abandoned mint building. He found the machinery rusty but mostly salvageable. All usable instruments and machines were shipped to the U.S. Mint in Philadelphia. The inspector reported that the building itself was in reasonably good condition.

Unsuccessful attempts were made to reopen the Dahlonega Mint, but the federal government had no further use for the structure. It offered both the Dahlonega and Charlotte Branch Mints for sale but declined to sell the Dahlonega Mint for the highest bid of only $1,525. A portion of the building was used for a short time as a school established for black children by the Freedmen's Bureau. After that, it remained empty until Congress donated it for use as North Georgia Agricultural College.

# 4

# Dahlonega during the Civil War

## THE SECESSION CONVENTION

As relations between the North and the South continued to deteriorate over the contentious issues of slavery, tariffs and states' rights, Georgia followed other Southern states in holding a Secession Convention. When the first vote was taken at the State Capitol in Milledgeville in January of 1861, there were 165 who cast their ballots for immediate secession and 150 who were opposed.

Both delegates representing Lumpkin County voted "Nay." There were few slave owners in the mountains of north Georgia, and many people supported remaining within the Union. Dahlonega attorney William Martin offered a resolution that would allow the people of Georgia to vote on "secession or no secession," but his resolution was strongly voted down by the other delegates.

Lumpkin County's other delegate, Benjamin Hamilton, expressed his views in a letter written to a friend in Dahlonega, saying:

> *Yesterday the ordinance was put on its final passage and the vote stood 208 in favor of its passage and 89 opposed. I voted no. On tomorrow the ordinance will be presented for the signatures of the members of the convention and I think from the arguments that are being used and the efforts being made that nearly all the members will sign it. I shall not sign it...The action of Georgia and the other seceding states is the only instance in the history of the world where a free and independent people have voted revolution. Surely madness rules the day...War with all its horrors and heavy poisons is upon us, and all to gratify a few ambitious men...*

## LUMPKIN COUNTY SOLDIERS OFF TO WAR

When President Lincoln issued a proclamation announcing an insurrection and calling for troops to be raised in the North, many formerly pro-Union people rallied to the Southern cause. Young men volunteered eagerly for military service to protect Southern women and homes from the Northern invaders. Lumpkin County's first unit to depart was the Dahlonega Volunteers. After being presented with a silk Confederate flag from the young ladies of Dahlonega, the recruits marched out of town to the sound of anvils being beaten in a parting salute.

A second company of volunteers was organized in June of 1861 under the command of Captain Joseph Hamilton, a graduate of West Point. The name these young men chose for their unit was the Blue Ridge Rifles. An article about their departure in the *Dahlonega Signal* noted, "No company from the state is better qualified for destructiveness, as they have been from their earliest boyhood used to the rifle and shut one eye when they shoot, and every time they pull the trigger a man will fall."

While many Lumpkin County men were enlisting in the Dahlonega Volunteers, the Blue Ridge Rifles and other Confederate units, there were others whose consciences led them to make their way over the mountains to join Union forces. Still others enlisted in the Georgia State Line, popularly known as Joe Brown's Army.

Governor Joseph E. Brown was concerned that Confederate troops could not be depended upon to defend the people of Georgia and consequently created an army of his own. A special company of state troops was assigned to guard the bridges of the Western & Atlantic Railroad, known as the State Road, which was a communication and materiel lifeline between Atlanta and Chattanooga.

Amory Dexter, a mining engineer who had come to Dahlonega from Boston in 1858, made a terse entry in his diary on June 6, 1861, noting, "Mint closed 1st June...U.S. Mail stopped June 1st." Four months later on November 14, he wrote, "we got the mill running for the first time," but by this time he was no longer able to get funds from Boston for paying expenses and taxes. As more and more local men went off to war, Dexter went from lacking funds to pay workers to being unable to find able-bodied men to work.

## BUSHWHACKERS AND OUTLAWS

By early 1863, the mountains of north Georgia had become the hideout of a large number of marauding bands of outlaws who raided, looted and burned homes, even murdering the inhabitants. When Governor Brown was advised that a large band of these outlaws was reported to be marching toward Dahlonega, he ordered Captain Edward M. Galt to take command of a company of Georgia State Line troops recently raised in Lumpkin County and go to the village's defense.

Galt and his men reached Dahlonega on January 23, 1864, expecting to defend the community against an imminent attack. Before the soldiers' arrival, however, the few men remaining in the village—those excused from military service due to age or service in a public office—had already gone out to meet the armed band and persuaded them to spare the town.

With this crisis resolved, Galt and the State Line troops set out to "scour the mountains and arrest the insurgents." By early February they had rounded up six hundred Confederate deserters and sent them back to their regiments. Fifty-three civilian troublemakers had been arrested and were marched in chains to Atlanta. Among those apprehended was the notorious Jeff Anderson from Lumpkin County, leader of a band of bushwhackers known as the Bridge Burners, who harassed Confederate troops and civilians alike.

As Union General William T. Sherman began his Atlanta Campaign in May of 1864, many Lumpkin County soldiers were part of the Confederate and State Line forces attempting to block the Federal advance through Georgia. With his Confederate forces greatly outnumbered, General Joseph Johnston was forced to order retreat after retreat in order to prevent Sherman from making his hallmark flanking maneuver and attacking from the rear. Many brave Lumpkin County men died at the battles of New Hope Church, Kennesaw Mountain, Peachtree Creek and Atlanta.

Dahlonega's location in the mountains kept it from becoming a battlefield and suffering the destruction of Sherman's March through Georgia. However, the village was profoundly affected by the Civil War in many other ways. In addition to enduring the hardship and grief

*Opposite:* Sergeant William John Turner Hutcheson was a member of Lumpkin County's volunteer unit known as the Blue Ridge Rifles. *Courtesy of Jimmy Anderson.*

Captain Augustus "Gus" Boyd died gallantly at the Battle of Baker's Creek, Mississippi. *Courtesy of Jimmy Anderson.*

of losing husbands, fathers, brothers and sons, the women had to provide for themselves and their children at a time when very little was available due to Union blockades. Many learned to gather native plants to use both as food and medicine. Women who had smokehouses where meat had been salt-cured dug up the dirt and invented ways to extract the salt from it. One of the biggest problems was finding an able-bodied man to cut and deliver the firewood required for cooking and warmth.

## FEDERAL OCCUPATION

After Lee's surrender at Appomattox on April 9, 1865, Dahlonega was designated a military post as a result of a letter sent to Secretary of War Edwin Stanton. The following words were written by Union General J.H. Wilson: "I have just learned that the U.S. Branch mint at Dahlonega is in good order, all of the buildings and fixtures being complete. I have directed General Winslow to send an officer and a party of men to that place for the purpose of protecting the interests of the Government."

The first Federal troops to arrive occupied the Presbyterian church. A later detachment established their headquarters and barracks in the abandoned mint building. Strict discipline was maintained in the soldiers' behavior, and any townspeople arrested were confined in a dungeon created in the basement of the old mint.

Early in the spring of 1866, the women of Dahlonega made plans to honor the memory of the community's fallen soldiers by decorating their graves with flowers. That first Confederate Memorial Day—then called Decoration Day—began with a service held at the Methodist church. The address was given by Colonel Weir Boyd, a local lawyer who had volunteered for service in the Confederacy even though he was past forty. He was elected colonel of a unit popularly known as the Boyd Guards. Boyd's son Augustus died heroically at the Battle of Baker's Creek, Mississippi.

At the close of Colonel Boyd's address, those assembled filed out of the church and formed a procession to the cemetery, their arms laden with flowers. As they passed the former mint edifice, Union soldiers on duty there watched closely but made no move to stop the procession.

At Mount Hope Cemetery, another address was given by Colonel W.P. Price, who had recently returned to Dahlonega to offer his services in restoring order following the war. When he had "told the story of the glory of the men who wore the gray," women and children covered the graves with colorful flowers picked from numerous yards and gardens. Henry Awtry, noted for his fine tenor voice, concluded the ceremony by singing "Farewell, Mother." A Union officer who had followed the party to the cemetery reported to his commanding officer that he found nothing treasonous in the people's desire to remember and honor their fallen soldiers.

The citizens of Dahlonega learned to tolerate the Union soldiers during the years the men in blue uniforms occupied the village. However, most local folks rejoiced when the Federal troops received orders in 1869 to leave.

5

# Dahlonega's Former Mint Becomes a College

## THE ESTABLISHMENT OF NORTH GEORGIA AGRICULTURAL COLLEGE

The mint building that had once hummed with the noise of coin stamps and presses again grew silent after the departure of the occupying Federal troops in 1869. One of Dahlonega's native sons, Colonel William P. Price, lamented the abandonment of such a fine structure and wondered if there could be some way it could be put to use for educational purposes. He was convinced that education was the best means for improving the quality of life in the north Georgia mountains and dedicated his life to that purpose.

The opportunity came in 1870 when Price was elected to Congress. He worked closely with Georgia Senator Joshua Hill to introduce a bill authorizing the secretary of the U.S. Treasury to convey the United States Branch Mint at Dahlonega to a recently incorporated school named North Georgia Agricultural College. The bill passed the Senate and House and was signed by President Ulysses S. Grant on April 20, 1871.

The trustees of the new college found themselves in possession of a building but with no funds for making needed repairs or hiring teachers. In order to receive needed financial assistance, they agreed for the school to become part of the University of Georgia. Colonel Price donated $4,000 and several lots in Dahlonega to help the college get started.

Although classes had begun the previous September, North Georgia Agricultural College officially opened its doors on January 6, 1873, with the invitation, "Whosoever will, may come." It was the second public college in the state and the first to admit female students. Women were not admitted at the University of Georgia until 1918.

Commenting on the college's coeducational policy, Dahlonega's *Mountain Signal* noted, "In undertaking the work of education upon a higher basis for the children of upper Georgia, our Board were unanimously of the opinion that both sexes should have equal advantage in this school. Such now appears to be the genius and spirit of the age."

A year later the *Mountain Signal* reported that more than two hundred students had attended the college in the past year, of which nearly half were female. The newspaper also noted that more than twelve hundred children in rural districts had been given summer school instruction by NGAC students. By July 24, 1875, the *Signal* could proclaim that "North Georgia Agricultural College is no longer an experiment but a grand success."

Notices advertised "FREE EDUCATION" at NGAC, with only a $5 entrance fee per five-month session. The notices also stated that "the healthfulness of the climate and cheapness of board make NGAC a desirable school for young men and women from those sections of the state visited with chills and fever." Other advertisements pointed out "the entire absence of temptations to vice which its location affords."

There were only two faculty members for the first term, but two students were hired to teach the preparatory department. A sub-freshman class was a necessity, as there were no public high schools in Georgia at that time. The president of the college, David W. Lewis, taught English and Greek. Benjamin P. Gaillard, professor of mathematics, Latin and natural sciences, began teaching the second term and would remain on the faculty until 1933. During that long tenure, he served twice as acting president of the institution and also as vice-president.

Like other land grant colleges founded by funds from the Morrill Act, NGAC was required to offer courses in military science designed to train young men to serve their country. The war department had promised to supply the college with military equipment as soon as there were 150 male students. The equipment, which included 150 Springfield Cadet Rifles, was received on campus in December of 1876. Lieutenant Joseph Garrard arrived shortly after the first of the year to take charge of the military department.

In what was probably the earliest "cooperative education" plan in Georgia, a "Normal Department" was added at NGAC in 1877. This enabled students to alternate teaching in the rural one-room schools with continuing their own academic studies during times when children were out of school helping plant and harvest the fields.

NGAC held its first graduation in June of 1878. The graduating class of twelve included Miss Willie Lewis, daughter of President David Lewis. Even though she had completed all the same course work as the male students, Chancellor Patrick H. Mell, who had come from the University of Georgia to present the diplomas, was reluctant to award a bachelor's degree to a female. He finally did so only after remembering that the university had awarded such a degree to an older married man a few years previously. He reasoned that if a married man could be called a "bachelor," so could a young woman!

The name, North Georgia Agricultural College, did not adequately describe this liberal arts institution that was both essentially military and coeducational. The pragmatic courses taught by the agricultural department were instrumental in the economic rehabilitation of the region, but they formed only a small portion of the school's curriculum. NGAC's School of Mining Engineering was one of the best in the nation and male graduates were commissioned into the United States Army with the same rank as those from West Point.

*Opposite:* Professor B.P. Gaillard taught at NGAC from 1873 until 1933 and served twice as acting president of the institution. *Courtesy of Jimmy Anderson.*

NGAC cadets displaying new uniforms and rifles in front of the former mint building circa 1877. *Courtesy of former NGCSU President Sherman Day.*

Members of the first graduating class at NGAC in 1878 included Miss Willie Lewis, daughter of President David Lewis. *Courtesy of the Georgia Department of Archives and History.*

NGAC's practical and inclusive approach to education led to such phenomenal growth that it exceeded the university in enrollment within a few years. Six months after its first graduation, however, tragedy struck without warning.

## DESTRUCTION BY FIRE

Shortly after midnight on the morning of December 20, 1878, President Lewis and his family awakened to the smell of smoke and cries of "Fire!" The Lewises and other faculty members and students who resided in the twenty-seven-room former mint building groped their way down the stairs to safety. Some cadets attempted to save books from President Lewis's extensive library, which he had donated to the college, by throwing them out the second-story windows, although many were damaged in the process.

The fire had apparently originated in the classroom wing, which was unoccupied at night, and the flames went undetected until a substantial portion of the structure was ablaze. There was no loss of life, but the college's only building lay in ruins. Also destroyed in the fire were the school's library, instruments and equipment, as well as the personal possessions of those living in the former mint edifice. To make matters even worse, the insurance policy carried on the building by the state had been allowed to lapse.

A vivid account of the impact of the fire appeared in the December 24 issue of Atlanta's *Daily Constitution* under the headline "North Georgia's Great Calamity": "The recent burning of the North Georgia Agricultural College is justly considered a misfortune to the whole state. It affects northeast Georgia as a peculiar calamity. Full accounts of the burning which come from Dahlonega state that the destruction was almost total, and that the remains of the well-equipped institution are blackened walls and smouldering ruins."

## RISING FROM THE ASHES

Before the ashes were cold, a meeting was held in the courthouse to make plans for rebuilding. Trustees, professors, students and local citizens resolved that the college must not die. Classes were not suspended even temporarily but were held in the old Dahlonega Academy, the courthouse and the churches. Less than two months after the disastrous fire, the editor of the *Signal* wrote, "The flocking of such a large number of students to the North Georgia College presents a strange phenomenon. They come every day just like the grand old building had never been wrapped in flames...It was feared that the students would go away and not return. But nothing of the sort has happened. The...exercises go on as if the fiery fiend had never been in our midst. And it really looks as if two new students had already taken the place of every one who had gone away."

Four months after the fire, plans had been drawn for a new building and bids from contractors were coming in. The cornerstone of the new structure was laid with Masonic ceremonies on June 25, 1879. Colonel Price, president of the college's board of trustees, used his personal funds to begin the process of reconstruction, and many of Dahlonega's citizens followed his example by making generous contributions of their own.

The student body and faculty members gathered in front of Price Memorial Hall circa 1900 to be photographed. *Courtesy of the Georgia Department of Archives and History.*

Although erected on the original T-shaped, hand-hewn granite foundation of the mint edifice, the new structure was considerably different in appearance due to the addition of a lofty steeple. The brick walls were not covered with stucco as had been done on the mint and the second story rose to twice the height of the mint's twelve-foot ceilings. In the front of the building, the mint's plain square windows were replaced with five large Gothic arched windows, the tallest one in the center pointing gracefully upward to the bell tower.

On November 22, 1880, the *Dahlonega Signal* reported: "Our new college building when completed, will be one of the most commodious and imposing edifices in north Georgia. Four rooms are ready for use, which were occupied by the school on Monday last."

## THE COLLEGE'S GROWTH OVER THE YEARS

The college campus soon began to expand. Dahlonega gold provided the means to erect a new building in 1899 when Captain J.A. Bostwick of New York donated both the Calhoun

Bostwick Hall (left) was built in 1899 and named for the benefactor who donated valuable mining property to the college. It was destroyed by fire in 1912. *Courtesy of the Georgia Department of Archives and History.*

and Benning Mines to the college. Bostwick Hall had been in use just a little over a decade when it was destroyed in 1912 by fire caused by faulty wiring.

A frame dormitory for women was erected in 1901, followed by a dormitory for men ("the Barracks") in 1903. An industrial building was constructed in 1913 to house the Electrical and Mining Engineering Department.

Students continued to enroll faster than dormitories could be built to house them; consequently, a number of cadets and coeds boarded with families in town. A new brick men's dormitory was named Barnes Hall to honor Professor J.C. "Daddy" Barnes, who not only taught mathematics but also ran the college farm, supervised the dormitories and dining hall, managed the finances and was engineer in charge of new construction during his half-century tenure from 1903 to 1950.

In the late 1920s there was a movement to change the name of the college due to confusion caused by the establishment of several agricultural colleges within the state. The first name proposed was Georgia State College, but North Georgia College was the name finally settled upon and legally adopted in 1930. The agriculture department was eliminated at that time, and arts and sciences became the major focus.

In 1931 all state educational institutions were brought under the control of a board of regents, which superseded the various boards of trustees that had previously administered the schools. This was the beginning of the University System of Georgia.

Colonel W.P. Price is considered the founding father of North Georgia College.
*Courtesy of North Georgia College & State University Archives.*

North Georgia College was reduced to a two-year college in 1933 when a number of schools were being closed due to the Great Depression. However, senior status was restored in 1948, at which time many former graduates of the junior college returned for two more years of study. The college quietly made history in 1973 by admitting females to the military program without any of the fuss and bother experienced years later by other military schools when they were required to admit women.

The college's first building, erected upon the foundation of the old mint, was named Price Memorial Hall in honor of the man considered to be the school's founder, Colonel W.P. Price. In celebration of the college's centennial in 1973, the tall bell tower was covered with gold from some of the same mines that yielded the precious metal coined on that site in years past.

The upper floor of Price Memorial was closed by the state fire marshal's office in the early 1980s because it was deemed a fire hazard. The entire building was vacated in 1994 in preparation for remodeling. Prior to the renovation work, college workmen removed all interior partitions added over the years, exposing the original floors, walls and ceilings for the first time in many decades. The astonishing revelation included the tops of tall arched doors and windows that had been hidden since the ceiling was lowered in years past to conserve heat. Also revealed were three beautiful cast-iron columns with Corinthian detailing at the tops.

Thanks to President Sherman Day's recognition of the historic significance of the building's original design, remodeling plans were altered to feature the graceful arches by using tray ceilings. Plexiglas was installed over a portion of the hand-hewn granite foundation in what had been the basement of the old mint building so that it remains permanently visible.

While all these changes were taking place within the school's hallmark building, a change in name was also occurring to reflect the institution's expanded status. In 1996 the school's name was officially changed to North Georgia College & State University (NGCSU).

## NGCSU TODAY

North Georgia College & State University today continues to expand and grow in many directions even as it remains deeply rooted in its original traditions and values. The school's focus on a well-rounded liberal arts education is combined with leadership training. In 2001–2002 NGCSU became the first university in Georgia to offer a minor in leadership, earning the designation The Leadership Institution of Georgia.

NGCSU is also The Military College of Georgia, one of only six senior military colleges in the nation and it takes pride in numbering thirty-six generals and admirals among its alumni.

Incoming freshmen at NGCSU have among the highest average SAT scores in the state, and the university consistently maintains one of the highest graduation rates in the University System of Georgia. Students also regularly attain the highest pass rate on state teaching certification exams.

In 2005 *Consumers Digest* declared NGCSU the fifth best value in public higher education in the nation. *U.S. News & World Report* ranked the institution as thirteenth in the South among public universities offering undergraduate and master's degrees. The university's first doctoral program (leading to a doctor of physical therapy degree) was initiated in 2006. The university's sixteenth president, Dr. David L. Potter, took office at NGCSU in January 2005. That fall semester the university set a new enrollment record of over 4,800 students, with more than 600 participating in the Corps of Cadets. North Georgia continues to expand off-campus programs, offering classes in Forsyth County, at Gainesville State College in Hall County and nursing classes in Cobb County.

The local campus continues to expand as the student body rapidly approaches five thousand. Building projects on the horizon include a new library and technology center, renovation of the education building, a new student recreation center and a parking deck. The new health and science building provides today's students with a modern facility and up-to-date equipment. Standing nearby, the school's oldest edifice—the beautifully remodeled Price Memorial Hall—is both an administration building and an architectural museum attesting to the vision and determination of the people who brought the college into being and would not let it die.

6

# Dahlonega's Popular Spa Porter Springs

## THE DISCOVERY OF A RICH MINERAL SPRING

During the seventeenth and eighteenth centuries mineral waters were believed to have many health-giving properties. When a mineral spring was discovered nine miles north of Dahlonega in 1868, it soon became a popular destination for those who came to drink and bathe in its waters in hopes of being cured of their ailments.

The spring was first discovered by Joseph McKee, a Methodist minister and land agent. He was traveling on foot through the north Georgia mountains when he stopped at a spring to assuage his thirst. Tasting the water, Reverend McKee immediately realized that it contained dissolved iron salts and made a careful note of its location at the foot of Cedar Mountain before continuing his journey. When he reached the home of Reverend William Tate about three miles away, he told his friend about the water's unusual taste and the reddish sediment clinging to the rocks, both characteristic of mineral water.

McKee and Tate later returned to the spring and dug it out to a depth of about three feet. In the process of removing the accumulated debris, they were surprised to find a wall of thin rocks surrounding the spring, "which would seem to indicate that the spring had been used for medical or other purposes, probably a thousand years ago," McKee reported.

Being a man of integrity, Reverend McKee went to Basil Porter, the owner of the property, and gave a full report about the spring's probable medicinal properties. As word spread and more and more people came to "take the waters," Porter began renting and selling small lots near the watering place now called Porter Springs. McKee and Tate both bought two lots each and built rental cabins on them.

Reverend McKee wrote an article about the spring for the *Methodist Advocate* in 1870. "The waters appear to be invested with extraordinary powers by a beneficent Creator," he wrote, "adapted to ameliorate and heal nearly all the diseases incident to mankind, especially chronic maladies which defy the skill of physicians." He went on to relate cases in which many people had been healed of numerous chronic ailments, including William Tate and his wife Sarah, who had previously been attended by "eleven physicians, none of whom could afford the least relief."

One of the most famous visitors to Porter Springs was Alexander Hamilton Stephens, former vice-president of the Confederacy, whose always frail health had further deteriorated during his imprisonment following the Civil War. Stephens was a U.S. Congressman from Georgia when he spent a week at the spa in the summer of 1873. He reported himself to have "considerably benefited" by taking the waters.

## THE QUEEN OF THE MOUNTAINS

Colonel Henry Patillo Farrow took time off from his duties as district attorney for the state of Georgia to spend the summer at Porter Springs in 1874 in hopes of getting relief from the rheumatism that plagued him. He was so impressed with the medicinal properties of the spring and its beautiful surroundings that he leased the property and began erecting buildings to house guests, but his construction could not keep pace with the spa's growing popularity. So many people were camping out on cots and pallets that Farrow had to advise hack drivers not to bring any more visitors until he could further expand his facilities.

And expand he did—in grand style. In addition to numerous rustic cottages, Colonel Farrow built a large U-shaped hotel, whose long front porches opened onto a beautifully landscaped quadrangular court where peacocks roamed freely. The dining room and ballroom were located in a separate building connected to the main building by an elevated walkway. This covered gangway could be quickly removed in case of fire and dynamite was kept on hand for this purpose.

Colonel Farrow advertised the property widely as "the Queen of the Mountains." An 1875 brochure boasted, "No such altitude and grand mountain scenery combined with waters of such medicinal value…can be found elsewhere in the South."

Advertised rates for room and board in 1888 were $22.50 per month, $8.00 per week and $1.50 per day. Hack fare from Gainesville was $2.00. The resort was open from June 1 to October 15 but closed during the cold months, as only a few rooms had fireplaces.

The resort soon became noted throughout the Southeast for its delicious and healthful cuisine. Colonel Farrow's well-kept garden, vineyard and orchard kept the kitchen supplied with fresh produce, and what couldn't be grown on the property was purchased from local farmers. A herd of Jersey cows provided milk and butter. Advertisements proclaimed that the chickens served in the Porter Springs dining room were not "worn out" like those served elsewhere but were "fat and healthy from never having been cooped up." An orchestra consisting of a violinist, bassist and harpist serenaded guests during meals and played for evening dances.

Numerous forms of recreation were provided for guests, including a tenpin alley, where they bowled with great wooden balls. Other popular attractions were the tennis courts, croquet grounds, swimming pool, fishing pond and a billiard table in the parlor. Mounts were provided for those who wanted to explore the area on horseback and hacks took others on sightseeing tours. Children played happily on swings and seesaws built for their entertainment. Hiking was a popular pastime for visitors of all ages, and if the weather happened to be rainy, guests could still take their daily constitutionals by walking on the covered porches. One round was exactly a quarter of a mile.

People from all over the state came to Porter Springs, hoping to benefit by drinking and bathing in its rich mineral water. *Courtesy of the author.*

Even though guests enjoyed all these delightful side attractions, the main reason for visiting the spa was its famed chalybeate (denoting the presence of iron) mineral spring. Pitchers of water were placed at strategic points around the hotel and guests were encouraged to drink as much as possible except at mealtimes, when it interfered with digestion. The pitchers were replenished with fresh water several times daily because mineral deposits settled to the bottom as unappealing brownish sediment after a few hours. The hotel had running water piped by gravity flow from a freestone spring on the hill behind the building, but servants had to carry the drinking water from the chalybeate spring.

Since mineral water was believed to be beneficial externally as well as internally, guests walked to the bathhouse, removed their clothes and pulled a plug out of a wooden trough overhead to release a flow of water. The spring water was ice cold even on the hottest summer day, and the squeals and gasps coming from the bathhouse when the plugs were pulled could be heard far and wide!

Guests loved hearing the colorful local legend about the Indian princess Trahlyta, who stayed youthful and beautiful by drinking from the spring and bathing in its waters. According to the tale, when Trahlyta was captured by the enemy warrior Wahsega and taken away from her "fountain of youth," she soon grew old and died. A remorseful Wahsega brought her body back to the base of Cedar Mountain for burial but was unable to locate the spring. A popular outing for guests at Porter Springs was to visit Trahlyta's grave located nearby and add a stone to the mound, which can still be seen today at the intersection of U.S. Highway 19 and GA Highway 60.

After Colonel Farrow's death in 1907, Porter Springs began to decline despite the efforts of his grandsons, Charlie and Henry Whitner, to keep the resort in operation. In later years others also attempted to restore it to its former state, but the Queen of the Mountains never regained the glory of her early years. The last time Porter Springs housed paying guests was in the late 1920s when two of Colonel Farrow's granddaughters reopened the resort for several summers as Trahlyta Lodge. However, family members continued to vacation there as long as the buildings were habitable.

Although deserted most of the time, the hotel still contained many of its original furnishings for many years, including a grand piano in the ballroom and another piano in the parlor. Even though this was still in an era when few people locked their doors, it became apparent that the old resort needed a caretaker to live on the premises and keep an eye on things. That's how Haley Edward Montague became the last resident in the old hotel.

When he was state executive director of the Young Men's Christian Association, Uncle Monty had brought many boys from the Atlanta YMCA to Porter Springs in his Model T Ford. They camped out in a big meadow they christened Camp Hardrock. He wasn't actually hired as a caretaker; he had just spent so much time at Porter Springs that when he retired, the Whitner family allowed him to live out the rest of his life in the setting he loved so much.

The Porter Springs Post Office was still in operation at that time and Mr. Montague became the postmaster. Everybody living in the district came to the hotel to get his or her mail. Sometimes they brought bottles and jars to fill with water from the mineral spring. However, most folks had lost their faith in the healing properties of mineral water by then.

By the time Mr. Montague died in 1958, much of the hotel was falling in and the Farrow heirs tore down the remainder. When the property was sold at public auction in 1962, some tracts were bought by Farrow heirs. Several others were bought by Edna Noblin and have since passed to her son, George David, the great-great-grandson of the man who first discovered Porter Springs, Reverend Joseph McKee.

Today nothing remains of the grand old resort once proudly referred to as the Queen of the Mountains, except for the spring itself and the stories still told of its vanished glory.

7

# DAHLONEGA'S POST–CIVIL WAR MINING BOOM

The Civil War had not been over long when gold mining resumed in Lumpkin County. Even though the placer deposits had played out, new methods for extracting veins of gold buried in the hillsides induced Northern capitalists to invest large sums of money to develop them. Hydraulic mining—using great jets of water to tear away the earth and expose the veins—had been used in the California gold rush and returning miners were eager to implement the technique in Lumpkin County.

## THE YAHOOLA DITCH

In order to bring water down to the mines with enough pressure to power the water cannons, the Boston-based Yahoola & Cane Creek Hydraulic Hose Mining Company had built an extensive aqueduct shortly before the outbreak of the Civil War. It was a monumental engineering feat. Although the dam was only seven miles from Dahlonega as the crow flies, the ditch more than doubled the distance in the process of following the curving contours of the mountainous terrain in order to maintain a constant rate of descent. Cuts had to be dug through hillsides and trestles were erected to carry the flumes over ravines.

An 1859 map shows two large trestles and five smaller ones. The "Long Tube," made of tongue-and-groove heart-pine boards held together by iron bands, was about three-quarters of a mile long. At its highest point, it was sixty-six feet above the valley floor.

The greatest difficulty was getting the water across the high bluffs on either side of Yahoola Creek just outside of Dahlonega, where the stream level is 250 feet below the town. The pre–Civil War solution was to build a high trestle almost 1,500 feet in length.

When the Boston company that originally built the aqueduct sent a young mining engineer named Frank W. Hall to Dahlonega in 1868 to inspect the prewar workings, he reported that the wooden trestles had rotted away. Rather than rebuild them, Hall piped the water down one side of a steep slope and up the opposite side in large iron tubes. A distinguished engineer from Boston insisted that the pipe could not withstand such pressure, but Hall made it work by doubling the thickness of the boiler iron at the bottom.

*Above:* The Yahoola Ditch was a hand-dug canal that brought water down to the mines with enough pressure to power water cannons for hydraulic mining. After the Civil War it was renamed the Hand Ditch for Nathan Hand, who repaired and extended it. *Courtesy of the Georgia Department of Archives and History.*

*Opposite above:* These miners use a hydraulic cannon to tear away the earth and expose hidden veins of gold. *Courtesy of the author.*

*Opposite below:* Long tubes took the place of trestles after the Civil War. Made of iron or heart-pine boards banded together, these tubes conveyed the water down one steep slope and up the opposite bank. *Courtesy of Enoch Hicks.*

Once the water was again flowing, Frank Hall's next assignment was to make extensive experiments to determine how the company's stamp mill could be improved to make it more efficient. The F.W. Hall Gold-Mill, which he patented, was soon widely used by many other mining companies.

The Yahoola & Cane Creek Hydraulic Hose Mining Company apparently lacked the capital to complete the repairs to the ditch. Its assets were seized by order of the Federal District Court in Atlanta and sold to satisfy debts owed to Frank W. Hall. The successful bidder at the August 1873 sale was an officer of the Yahoola Company named Nathan H. Hand.

Hand, a native of Ohio, incorporated the Hand Gold Mining Company in 1874 and acquired ownership of the right of way for the ditch (some 2,280 acres) as well as rights for "turning the waters of the Yahoola River and Cane Creek and diverting their waters from their natural channel." After he repaired and extended the Yahoola Ditch, it began to be known as the Hand Ditch.

By the time the Consolidated Gold Mining Company purchased the Hand Mine and Ditch in 1898, the canal was reported to be 32 miles long, with about 15 more miles of branches. It was described as being "3 feet deep, 5 feet wide at the bottom and 7 1/2 feet wide at the top." The Yahoola or Hand Ditch supplied water and generated electricity at the huge Consolidated plant, reported to be the largest ever constructed east of the Mississippi River.

## THE DAHLONEGA METHOD

In 1879 *Harper's New Monthly Magazine* sent a writer to Dahlonega to do research for an article entitled "Gold Mining in Georgia." The article, which appeared in the September issue, provides wonderful eyewitness descriptions of scenes long vanished in time, such as "the ruins of the old United States Mint, looking very romantic in the sunset glow." An artist also illustrated the scenes with fine pen-and-ink drawings. One of the most dramatic illustrations shows great torrents of water released from a reservoir at the top of the ridge sweeping ore down a steep hillside to be processed in the mill below. This technique was developed locally and called the Dahlonega Method.

The anonymous *Harper's* writer described it vividly:

> *This operation is called "flooding" the mine, and one evening we rode out to the Findley Mine to see it. There the cut runs straight up and down the side of a hill 500 feet high, and is in the form of a deep, irregular vertical trench...We climbed to the summit of a high knoll jutting up by the line of the cut, and waited. In a moment an ominous "grumble and rumble and roar" was heard, which, beginning faint and far aloft, gradually grew more threatening, until there was a sudden volley of sound, and at the end of the narrow trench a mighty mass of red-brown waters came leaping over the ledge...But it was not all water, nor even mud. Tons upon tons of broken rocks were coming down through this terrible flume, rolling over and over, rattling among their fellows, grinding along the walls, bounding out of the narrow crevice, leaping high above the red spray, and falling in ringing rain upon the stony floor. The noise was a hoarse, crushing, terrific roar. The force was prodigious.*

## EARLY HYDROELECTRIC POWER IN LUMPKIN COUNTY

It is a little known fact that some of the earliest use of hydroelectric power in the United States was generated from the waters of the Chestatee River in Lumpkin County. In 1886 the Garnet Waterpower & Mining Company of New York City built a mining plant at the Garnet Mine, located seven miles northeast of Dahlonega. It included two large turbine wheels to run the pump and the mill, a forty-horsepower engine and boiler and a small dynamo for furnishing light. The entire power taken from the river to operate the mill was two hundred horsepower.

This early use of hydroelectric power on the Chestatee took place only four years after the nation's first hydroelectric power plant began operations on the Fox River near Appleton, Wisconsin, on September 30, 1882. Prior to that time coal was the only fuel used to produce electricity.

The Dahlonega Method, also called "flooding the mine," was dramatically described by a writer sent to Dahlonega in 1879 from *Harper's New Monthly Magazine. Courtesy of the Dahlonega Gold Museum.*

In the March 13, 1884 issue of the *Dahlonega Nugget*, Editor R.B. King wrote: "Electricity, although but recently adapted to mechanical purposes, already gives indications of its universal application by the variety of uses to which it may be applied. Already in mining operations it is being utilized and furnishes light, a means of blasting, and in the telephone, a satisfactory method of communication between different parts of extensive underground operations. These, doubtless, are but the beginning of its usefulness and service."

## THE CHESTATEE MINING COMPANY

Northern capitalists were quick to see how the development of hydroelectric power could be used to expedite the gold mining process. In 1893 the Chestatee Mining Company, "composed largely of gentlemen of means from St. Louis, Missouri," began operations on the Chestatee several miles south of Dahlonega, where the Highway 60 bridge now crosses the river.

The Chestatee Mining Company's plan was to cut a new channel for the river and divert it in order to work the original riverbed for gold. Their plant included two sixty-six-inch Leffel turbine water wheels. One of the turbines powered the main pump; the other actuated the fifty-horsepower generator, which furnished electricity to the twenty-five-horsepower electric motor and a small motor used for pumping water from the river. The plant was designed to work around the clock, using the electric generator to furnish light as well as power.

After excavating the new channel and turning the river, the disappointed miners found relatively little gold in the dry bed. The company abandoned operations and sold the property for a comparatively small sum. Today the river flows through both channels, and golfers from the Birch River Golf Course endeavor to place their balls into holes number four and five on the island without landing in the Chestatee.

## THE CROWN MOUNTAIN MINING AND MILLING COMPANY

Crown Mountain, a ridge of land located just south of Dahlonega, was speculated to be the mother lode where all gold veins and leads in the area originated. Until the development of electricity, however, gold there was inaccessible due to lack of water power needed to mine it.

In 1900 the Crown Mountain Mining and Milling Company built a hydroelectric plant on the headwaters of the Chestatee River twelve miles north of Dahlonega above Turner's Corner. Water was channeled into an 8-foot canal at Seabolt Shoals on Waters Creek and at Cannon Falls on Frogtown Creek. About 250 feet above the plant, the water went into a huge wooden tube. The canals and tube provided a perpendicular fall of 95 feet with a flow of about 9,000 cubic feet of water per minute, sufficient to generate over 1500 horsepower.

Power lines conveyed electricity generated at the Seabolt Shoals plant to a sixty-stamp mill constructed at the base of Crown Mountain. In addition to operating the mill, the electricity was also used to pump water from the Chestatee River to a reservoir on top of the mountain.

In the May 18, 1900 issue of the *Dahlonega Nugget*, Editor W.B. Townsend wrote: "The development of this power will bring home to us the wonders of the greatest modern discovery—the transmission of power by a single wire ten miles without appreciable loss. Thirty years ago such a proposition would have been ridiculed...Now power is being transmitted fifty miles with little loss." Editor Townsend furnished his readers with weekly reports of progress made. On February 1, 1901, he gave the following account: "The Crown Mountain machinery is arriving in large quantities at Gainesville and is being hauled over

The mill of the Crown Mountain Mining Company was run by electricity generated at power plants on the Chestatee River in the early 1900s. *Courtesy of the Georgia Department of Archives and History.*

as fast as the roads permit…The big pump that will supply water to the reservoir on top of Crown Mountain…is the largest ever brought to the gold region. It will be driven by a 300-horsepower motor."

In the July 19, 1901 issue, Townsend described how "the electric button was touched and the great pump…set to running, forcing the waters of the Chestatee River more than 500 feet to the top of the mountain for the purpose of robbing it of its precious metals." He went on to note that "many people came out to see the spectacle and marvel how little wires could transmit enough power fourteen miles to run the gigantic machinery."

## GORGE DAM POWER PLANT

When the Seabolt Shoals plant was unable to generate sufficient power to run the mining operation during the dry season, the Crown Mountain Mining and Milling Company began work on another hydroelectric plant in 1902. Because the rock-filled log-crib dam was built at a place where the Chestatee narrows between high cliffs, this plant soon became known as the Gorge Dam Power Plant. Editor Townsend described the completed dam as being "41 feet high and 290 feet wide," although the actual channel of the river was only 35 feet across.

The dam was carefully designed to withstand the tremendous pressure of the periodic floods for which the Chestatee River is noted, but a third of it was washed away by the destructive freshet of 1906. By this time the Crown Mountain plant had already shut down and the dam was never rebuilt.

The Gorge Dam and Power Plant were built in 1902 to generate electricity for pumping water from the Chestatee River to the top of Crown Mountain for hydraulic mining. Although designed to withstand floods, the rock-filled log-crib dam was washed out by the freshet of 1906. *Courtesy of the Georgia Department of Archives and History.*

## THE NEW BRIDGE POWER PLANT OF THE GAINESVILLE AND DAHLONEGA ELECTRIC RAILROAD COMPANY

Ever since a railroad had been built in 1871 to link Gainesville with Atlanta, there had been talk of extending the line from Gainesville to Dahlonega. Colonel W.P. Price was one of the strongest proponents. As a state legislator and United States Congressman, his frequent travels made him very aware of the need for better transportation to Dahlonega. He was so eager to have a railroad that he used his own money to have a survey made to acquire the right of way. His plan was to finance it by selling scrip that could later be exchanged for both freight and passenger fares.

When the surveyors appeared on the outskirts of Dahlonega in 1879, many people turned out to celebrate the driving of the last stake, expecting to return to the same spot a year later to welcome the first train. That eagerly anticipated event never took place, even though a railroad bridge was built across the Chattahoochee River outside Gainesville and the right of way was graded to the Lumpkin County line.

Editorials in the local newspaper enjoined citizens to dig deep into their pockets for funds to complete the railroad, promising that when it was built, "farmers would be able to get their produce to market more efficiently, merchants could afford to sell their wares a fourth cheaper, taxes would go down, land prices would double within a year, the mines would be given new impetus, and the town and college would soon double in size."

An 1884 article noted that Lumpkin County and Dahlonega were "in the midst of a financial dearth" and that it was "the duty of every citizen to aid in the building of a railroad to boost the economy." Despite the ongoing efforts of Colonel Price and other railroad proponents, no train whistle was heard. In 1900 Colonel Price stated his willingness to donate his "unfinished track including the piers at the Chattahoochee River with all of his road and $500 besides" to a new company that was proposing to solicit subscriptions and complete the road.

The Gainesville and Dahlonega Electric Railroad Company was headed by a former Union general named A.J. Warner, who was noted for his experience in developing mining properties as well as building railroads. Warner, founder of the North Georgia Electric Company as well as the Gainesville & Dahlonega Electric Railway Company, and his associates were so optimistic about the future of hydroelectric development in north Georgia that they bought up many water power properties between 1902 and 1905. These two companies were the predecessors of Georgia Power Company.

Warner's company soon began work on a twelve-hundred-horsepower hydroelectric plant located on the Chestatee River at the place called New Bridge (formerly Leather's Ford). Half the power generated was intended to run the electric railroad between Gainesville and Dahlonega; the other half was conveyed fifteen miles on heavy copper wires to Gainesville to power the city's electric streetcars and street lamps. It also provided lighting for hotels and other places of business.

With the building of the dam and power plant at New Bridge, it seemed certain that the railroad was finally coming to Dahlonega. Yet in April of 1905, the stockholders of the Gainesville and Dahlonega Electric Railway Company sold all of their holdings. The following January, the editor of the *Dahlonega Nugget* wrote, "For years the citizens of Dahlonega have been expecting and patiently waiting for a railroad to be built from Gainesville, but becoming tired of so much talk and nothing done, they have decided to turn their attention in another direction and see if one from Roswell or Atlanta cannot be put through at an early date."

The iron horse never made it to Dahlonega despite great effort and financial outlay on the part of Colonel Price and numerous others. Sidney O. Smith, great-grandson of Colonel W.P. Price, believes that it was the advent of the automobile in the early 1900s that drove the final nail in the coffin of Dahlonega's long-anticipated railroad.

The power plant of the Gainesville and Dahlonega Electric Railway Company at New Bridge operated from 1902 until 1927. By that time its equipment was outdated and in poor repair, and the rotting timbers in the two-hundred-foot-long dam gradually washed out over the years. The area was submerged beneath the waters of Lake Lanier in the 1950s when Buford Dam backed up the Chattahoochee River.

## OTHER HYDROELECTRIC POWER PLANTS IN LUMPKIN COUNTY

The last hydroelectric plant on the Chestatee River was built in 1917 to provide power for mining and milling pyrites to make sulfuric acid for munitions during World War I. The dam,

The wheel and power plant at Cane Creek Falls generated electricity for Dahlonega from 1921 to 1931. *Courtesy of the Georgia Department of Archives and History.*

power plant and mill had been in operation only a short time when the war ended. With pyrites no longer in demand, the operation switched to quarrying rock for road building. The power plant continued to generate electricity for the surrounding area for several years after the quarry shut down in 1929.

Not all hydroelectric power generated in Lumpkin County came from the Chestatee River. The huge mill of the Consolidated Gold Mines built in 1900 was powered by the headwaters of Yahoola Creek, brought down through the mountains by means of a twenty-mile aqueduct called the Hand Ditch and stored in a reservoir above the mill.

A four-foot wooden tube conveyed the water to two five-hundred-horsepower Pelton wheels, each of which was capable of running the mill. One dynamo furnished electricity for operating the ore tram cars and running the chlorination plant. A second dynamo generated power for electric lights, not only for the mill and mines but also for businesses, residences and the college in Dahlonega.

After the Consolidated Gold Mining Company went bankrupt in 1905 and shut down operations, the dynamo continued to provide the town with electricity until the Hand Ditch sprang so many leaks that there was no longer enough water to generate power. Dahlonega was without electric lights until 1921, when Robert Howser installed a water wheel and power plant at Cane Creek Falls, which generated electricity for the next decade. This huge wheel was reportedly the second most powerful overshot wheel ever used in the United States. It was dismantled and sold for scrap metal at the beginning of World War II.

# 8

# Dahlonega during the First Half of the Twentieth Century

## THE CONSOLIDATED GOLD MINING COMPANY AND THE LAST BIG MINING BOOM

State Geologist W.S. Yeates's 1896 report on the gold deposits of Georgia generated a great deal of renewed interest in Lumpkin County's mines. Northern capitalists and mining experts came to inspect the best-known gold properties and determined that enough gold remained to turn a profit if extracted with the most up-to-date methods.

In late 1898 the Dahlonega Consolidated Gold Mining Company was organized with a capital stock of $5 million and began purchasing a number of well-known mines. Construction was begun on a huge processing plant, which included a mill with a hundred and twenty stamps to crush the hard rock ore. The Consolidated Company also erected a chlorination plant that would supposedly save 95 percent of the gold, thus making it profitable to work even low-grade ore. The plant was reported to be the largest ever constructed east of the Mississippi River.

A huge rock crusher weighing eighteen thousand pounds was shipped to Gainesville by rail and then hauled twenty-five miles to Dahlonega on a wagon with six-inch-wide steel tires. It was moved by sixteen mules—twelve pulling and four pushing—a journey requiring four days.

"There is no calculating the amount of good the Dahlonega Consolidated Gold Mining Company is doing in this country: every industrious laborer with or without a team is given employment, getting the mines ready for successful operation," wrote the editor of the June 30, 1899 *Dahlonega Nugget*. He also noted that Western miners were "utterly astounded in both the quantity and quality of ore in Lumpkin county and the cheapness with which it can be handled."

On December 14, 1900, Editor Townsend described a recent visit to "the Consolidated Company's big mining works," saying, "We started at a point where the ore is dumped into the crusher and went down into the mill where the gold is caught on the plates, and from there to the tunnel which is being driven to strike the large sixteen foot vein." Apparently the

The Consolidated Gold Mining Company built what was reportedly the largest gold mining plant ever constructed east of the Mississippi River. It began operations in 1900 but was bankrupt by 1906. *Courtesy of the Consolidated Gold Mine.*

An 18,000-pound rock crusher for the Consolidated mill was hauled to Dahlonega on a wagon moved by sixteen mules, twelve pulling and four pushing. *Courtesy of the Georgia Department of Archives and History.*

Early automobiles are shown on the south side of the Dahlonega Public Square. *Courtesy of Hal Williams.*

Consolidated Company's expectations far exceeded the amount of gold available. In 1906 the property was sold at a trustees' sale and bid off for a mere $20,000. The buildings stood abandoned, an impressive but expensive ruin. "The company went broke because they just plain ran out of ore to process," explained Marion Boatfield, who, with her husband John, lived on the property for a number of years.

## NO LICENSE NEEDED TO DRIVE EARLY AUTOMOBILES

The more Dahlonega residents heard about the new "horseless carriages" that were replacing horses and buggies as modes of transportation, the more the Meaders brothers wanted to acquire one of those newfangled inventions for themselves. They saved up their money and traveled to Atlanta in late May of 1906.

Frank was eager to drive their new Rambler to Dahlonega, but Bob needed to get home sooner, so he caught the train to Gainesville and hired a horse and buggy from a livery stable for the remainder of the journey. When Frank reached the outskirts of town, Bob met him with a team of horses to help the automobile ascend the long steep hill.

When they reached the top of the hill just beyond the college, Frank asked, "Is there anybody in town watching for our arrival?" "The square is full of people," Bob assured him. "Then untie the horses," Frank told his brother. "I'm gonna drive this thing into town or tear it up!"

Frank proudly drove his new Rambler into town to the excitement and cheers of all the citizens gathered on the Public Square. This was the first automobile that most folks in Dahlonega had ever seen.

It wasn't long before others acquired cars as well. Will Jones's store was for a time the only place in town to buy gas, which was hauled into Dahlonega in big tanks on a wagon pulled by two black mules.

"My daddy, Dr. S.A. West, used his old black Model T Ford to visit his patients out in the country and in neighboring counties," the late Harold West related in an interview. "I would often go on rounds with him and drive the car for him. In those days there was no age limit on driving, and you didn't even have to have a license. If you could afford a car, you could drive it. I started learning to drive when I was six years old."

## "NUMBER, PLEASE"

When telephones first became available, the Southern Bell Telephone Company did not install its long distance lines but contracted the work. Bob Meaders heard that the company had advertised for bids to build a line from Atlanta to Macon and decided to submit a bid, even though he knew nothing about telephones or telephone lines.

He soon received a letter asking him to come to the Atlanta office, where the president of the company suggested that he revise his bid. Meaders refused, saying he could do the job for his bid but not a penny less. As it turned out, his bid was half the amount of the next lowest bid!

All the other bidders had presidents, construction superintendents, fancy offices and stenographers. Since Meaders had only mule teams, wagons and a few workmen, he could afford to do the job for less. When Southern Bell awarded him the contract, Bob started digging holes and raising poles. He then bought himself some spurs and practiced climbing the poles so he would be ready when it came time to attach the telephone wires to glass insulators on the tops.

Dahlonega's first telephone exchange was located in the building on the right, known as Meaders' Corner. *Courtesy of the author.*

After successfully completing the contract, Bob was told that the company would do their own construction in the future. When he was offered the position of construction superintendent, he turned it down because he didn't think there was much future in the job.

Not long after that a Western Electric Company salesman came to Dahlonega and attempted to sell Meaders a telephone exchange. "People in our small town wouldn't bother using a telephone," he was told. However, Bob finally agreed that if they could get a hundred subscribers, he would make the purchase. By ten o'clock the next morning the salesman had the necessary subscribers. Three months after the exchange went into operation, it was inadequate and had to be swapped for a larger one.

Older citizens can remember hand-cranking their telephones and hearing the operator come on the line saying, "Number, please." The person operating the exchange then inserted the caller's plug into the proper socket, pulled the toggle back and hand cranked the desired number. Sometimes, however, the woman known to most callers only as "Central" would inform the caller that so-and-so was not home and relate his or her current whereabouts. From her location on the second floor of the Meaders building on the northeast corner of the Public Square, Central kept a watchful eye and knew who had gone into Moore's store, who was just coming out of Woody's Barber Shop and who was still in the courthouse!

## EARLY SILENT MOVIES FILMED IN DAHLONEGA

During the decades of the nineteenth century when Lumpkin County miners were busy developing new ways to extract gold from the earth, numerous experiments were taking place elsewhere to create an interesting phenomenon called moving pictures. Most of these were in Europe, but they did not go unnoticed in America.

By 1891 Thomas A. Edison, who had already invented the electric light bulb and the phonograph, applied for a patent for a Kinetograph camera and Kinetoscope viewing box. Edison's Kinetoscope (from the Greek *kinetos*, meaning "to move," and *scopein*, meaning "to view") made its debut in London in 1894. Some very brief silent films were made during the following years, including the fifteen-minute epic fantasy *Voyage to the Moon* in 1902.

Films gradually became longer and more sophisticated as well as increasingly popular on both sides of the Atlantic. The first film companies in the United States were based in New York. When Fox Film Company decided to make a movie based on the best-selling western novel entitled *The Plunderer*, they needed a location that offered abandoned gold mines, mining cuts and rugged mountain scenery. Transporting all the actors and equipment to a Western state was an expensive proposition, so the director was delighted to learn about a place called Dahlonega, Georgia, that offered the same type of setting.

After reaching Gainesville—just over a day's journey from New York by train—the film crew hired wagons to haul their baggage the remaining twenty-five miles to Dahlonega. There they were provided with comfortable accommodations at the Mountain Inn. This large hotel overlooking the town had been erected a few years earlier by the Consolidated Gold Mining Company. The proprietor, Dr. Craig Arnold, treated his guests to a lavish table of Southern cooking.

In addition to housing and feeding the actors, Dr. Arnold assisted Director Edgar Lewis in locating suitable backgrounds and local people to use as extras. In addition to the thrill

Originally built circa 1900 by the ill-fated Consolidated Gold Mining Company, the Mountain Inn hosted Fox Film's director and cast during the filming of *The Plunderer* in 1915. *Courtesy of the author.*

of being in a movie, extras were paid $1.00 per morning and $1.50 if they worked into the afternoon. Arnold himself played the role of a wealthy mine owner.

Much of the filming took place on the site of the Consolidated mining and milling plant, which had been abandoned since the company went bankrupt in 1906. The former commissary building was converted into a dance hall for the story and was the setting for a rip-roaring scene in which a fight breaks out between drunken miners, causing a hanging lamp to fall to the floor and explode.

Leading man William Farnum played one of the owners of a fabulous mine known in the movie as the Cross of Gold. Editor W.B. Townsend couldn't resist writing in the April 1, 1915 issue of the *Dahlonega Nugget* that "one of the actors [obviously referring to Farnum] gets a salary higher than paid the President of the United States."

Townsend went on to say, "This picture will spread the fame of Dahlonega over the entire world and show the natural beauty of our mountains, the many large open cuts where gold was taken in years past and create a renewed interest in gold mining."

Five other silent movies were filmed in Dahlonega over the next few years, including *The Daughter of Devil Dan*, which created some excitement not in the script. Leading lady Irma Harrison was pleading with her father, Devil Dan, to give up his illegal manufacture of whiskey. The script then required that she blow up the dam upstream to remove all traces of the still before her sweetheart arrived to arrest the moonshiners. All at once, a real bullet was fired and a real U.S. marshal crashed the scene and arrested the whole cast. No amount of explaining could convince the officer that they weren't really moonshiners, and the whole company had to appear in the federal court at Gainesville!

Numerous efforts have been made to locate these historic films, but they were apparently destroyed in a film warehouse fire many years ago.

An early silent movie entitled *The Plunderer* was filmed in and around Dahlonega in 1915. *Photo taken by Henry W. Moore, courtesy of Mrs. Henry W. Moore.*

## GETTING CORN OFF THE COB AND INTO THE JUG

Corn was for many years the major crop harvested in Lumpkin County, but it didn't bring much income at market in its natural state. Therefore it became common practice to convert corn into a form that was easier to transport and commanded a higher price. "Moonshine" was the only cash crop many farmers made and their only means of paying their taxes.

Making whiskey was a reputable and legal profession well into the twentieth century, and moonshiners took great pride in the quality of their liquor. It was common to bequeath gallons of homemade whiskey to descendants, along with wagons and mules and household items. Preachers were frequently paid in gallons of whiskey, for it was plentiful at a time when there was little cash in circulation.

Taxes were first levied on distilling alcohol in this country as a means of paying for the Revolutionary War. President Thomas Jefferson repealed the excise tax on whiskey, but it was restored after the Civil War, again as a means of paying war debts.

Agents responsible for arresting those making liquor without paying the required revenue to the government were called "revenuers." Men who continued to ply their trade without official sanction became known as "bootleggers," due to their practice of concealing a flask inside a high boot. The term "moonshining" referred to a product frequently made at night to escape detection.

One moonshiner feigned madness every time he was apprehended so he would be sent to the mental institution instead of jail. He was "crazy like a fox" because he knew he would be released from the insane asylum in three months, whereas the jail sentence for bootlegging was eight months!

Prohibition came into effect when the Eighteenth Amendment was passed in 1919, making it illegal to make or sell alcohol, with or without a license or paying tax. Instead of discouraging moonshining, however, Prohibition actually encouraged it in numerous instances. Limiting the supply caused the price to jump from one dollar to ten dollars per gallon—an increase many considered well worth the risk of a jail sentence.

Many of the mountaineers were descendants of Scotch-Irish pioneers who came to the New World in search of the freedom it promised, and they considered Prohibition to be a violation of their basic inalienable rights. They viewed making moonshine much the same as brewing coffee. If they got caught, they served their term, and when they got out, they went home and cranked up the still—all without any loss of standing in a community where half the population was at one time involved in making liquor.

The wood of American chestnut and sourwood trees was the preferred fuel for stills because it burned without making the telltale smoke that was a dead giveaway to revenuers. Moonshiners frequently kept a mule near their stills as an alarm system. Mules were reported to hear everything and when their ears started to twitch, the bootleggers knew to start running!

Even after Prohibition was repealed in 1933, the manufacture and sale of alcohol continued to be illegal without a government license. The cost of the required license—in addition to paying alcohol taxes—cut so deeply into profits that many mountaineers continued to bootleg.

In order to outrun the law to get their product to market without being arrested, moonshiners hired mechanics to soup up their engines and build suspension systems that could carry heavy loads undetected and handle sharp curves at high speeds. It was only when police cars were equipped with radios, enabling law enforcement agents to call ahead and set up roadblocks, that moonshining finally declined. The bootleggers' fast cars did not go to waste, however; they became the prototypes for stock car racing.

## LUMPKIN COUNTY PYRITES VITAL IN WORLD WAR I

When the United States entered World War I in the summer of 1917, 146 young men from Lumpkin County either volunteered or were drafted. More than 200 contributed to the war effort without leaving home: these men were working to build the mill of the Chestatee Pyrites and Chemical Corporation in eastern Lumpkin County.

Pyrites were in great demand for producing sulfuric acid needed for munitions during World War I. As more and more of the sources of European sulfur were cut off by the war, the government recognized the urgent need to develop the nation's own resources. Consequently, former state geologist N.P. Pratt was given a government contract to mine Lumpkin County pyrites and ship the ore to Copper Hill, Tennessee, to be smelted. The operation was considered so important that the men working at the mine were exempted from military duty.

The company's small fleet of trucks was inadequate to haul the huge volume of ore being extracted from the earth, so local farmers were paid $2 per ton to transport it seven miles to the railroad at Clermont. Since roads were often impassable during wet weather, work was begun on a railroad spur line from Clermont to the Chestatee Pyrites Mine.

The *Atlanta Constitution* published a lengthy article about the importance of Lumpkin County's pyrites deposits, not only to manufacture explosives vital to the war effort but also as a necessary element in the compounding of soil fertilizers. It noted that more known pyrites ore was located "within a stone's throw of Atlanta than in the rest of the U.S. combined."

Editor W.B. Townsend described his visit to the pyrites mine in the March 15, 1918 issue of the *Dahlonega Nugget*, noting the hum of machinery operated by a power plant on the Chestatee River and the sight of many men pushing ore cars in and out of the tunnel. "Work is progressing on the big mill as fast as possible with the hands obtainable," he reported, "but many more are needed badly." Townsend continued to give regular enthusiastic reports about the bustling activity at the Chestatee Pyrites Mine. On July 12, 1918, he wrote: "A busy town has sprung up bringing much life and prosperity into the country" and on September 18, he noted that the mill "runs both day and night, and not withstanding the scarcity of hands about two hundred tons of pyrites are turned out daily...More buildings will be erected for the accommodation of laborers who wish to locate there...Labor is the great problem now."

Fewer than two months later Editor Townsend reported, "The greatest war ever known came to a close last Monday." The termination of World War I also ended the need for large amounts of sulfuric acid for munitions, and the government canceled its contract with the Chestatee Pyrites and Chemical Company. Since N.P. Pratt and his brother George had invested enormous sums of money in developing the mine, they sued the government for breach of contract. They were eventually awarded a settlement of $459,000.

Even though the need for pyrites no longer existed, another use was found for the Chestatee plant. In 1920 the State Highway Commission made arrangements with the Pratts to quarry and crush stone for the paving of Highway 52—the first road to be paved in Lumpkin County.

During the years from 1921 to 1923, the new tunnel grew to massive proportions as its harder-than-granite "Blue Billy" rock was quarried to pave other highways. The stone-crushing plant was enlarged during 1926–1927, but operations were halted in the latter part of 1928

Pyrites mined in eastern Lumpkin County were in great demand for making explosives during World War I. Shown here are the railroad spur line tracks, the processing mill and the hoist house. *Courtesy of the Georgia Department of Archives and History.*

due to suspension of state highway work and added competition. The machinery and other equipment was sold and removed. Railroad tracks were purchased by Japan for scrap metal. Abandoned homes were torn down for lumber to be used elsewhere. Only gaping holes in the earth and the mill's massive concrete foundation remained of the once-bustling mining community, now an abandoned ghost town.

## "HOOVER DAYS"

Just as the prosperity brought to Lumpkin County by the pyrites mine was coming to an end, the stock market crashed and the nation spiraled downward into the Great Depression. Because President Herbert Hoover was in office at the time, he was made the scapegoat for the Depression, causing many people to refer to those days of economic desperation as the "Hoover Days."

Jobs and money were painfully scarce, and to make matters worse, the ground of many farms was becoming too poor to work. As a result a number of local men went to Ohio looking for jobs. The late Fred Hood remembered his experience vividly: "Work was so scarce in 1930 that I hitchhiked all the way up to Ohio trying to find a job. Sometimes I walked all day without catching a ride. Some nights I found a barn to sleep in; other nights I had to sleep on the ground. I never did find work up there so I hitchhiked back to Georgia a couple of weeks later."

According to his granddaughter, the late Rita Early, William A. Reid was more fortunate: "Grandpa worked in Akron [Ohio] for Goodyear for sixteen years, and he helped a number of people from Lumpkin County get jobs with Goodyear at a time when jobs were very scarce. He and Grandma Callie ran a boarding house, and many of the people he helped boarded with them."

The late Lillie Sanders and her husband Fred were both working at the Bank of Dahlonega when they heard on the radio that the president of the United States had ordered all the banks in the country to be closed on a day that came to be known as Black Tuesday.

"That was during the Depression when so many banks were failing," Lillie reminisced. "The Bank of Dahlonega was sound, however, and we saw no reason why we should close down. We opened the door at 9 a.m. as usual, but a few minutes later here came the sheriff and his deputy. They said that if we didn't lock the door, they would have to lock it for us. There was nothing to do but put all the money in the vault and go home...We didn't know how long we would have to stay closed, but as it turned out, the bank was allowed to reopen three days later for business as usual."

## THE CIVILIAN CONSERVATION CORPS

The year after he was elected president in 1932, Franklin Delano Roosevelt established the Civilian Conservation Corps—popularly known as the CCC—to create jobs and put money into local communities. Men accepted into the program wore surplus World War I clothing and lived in tents or rough wooden structures. They were paid $1 a day, of which they kept $5 a month and sent the remaining $25 to their families. Men who worked their way up in the ranks to become leaders were paid $36 a month.

The CCC (Civilian Conservation Corps) Camp F-2, located on the outskirts of Dahlonega circa 1932. *Courtesy of the Georgia Department of Archives and History.*

Lumpkin County had two CCC camps: Camp F-2 was located just north of town where the middle school is now located. Its purpose was primarily to provide useful work and vocational training for young men just starting out in life.

Camp F-11 was known as the Veterans' Camp because it was made up of World War I veterans, most of whom were over forty and had some sort of physical handicap. It was located ten miles north of town on a site that would later become a 4-H camp. Hoyt Brown drove the "road builder" when he was stationed at Camp F-11, but what he remembered most was when the CCC was sent to Gainesville in April of 1936 to search for bodies and clean up after a disastrous tornado that killed over two hundred people.

In addition to supporting themselves and their families, the men who were part of the CCC served their country by helping conserve natural resources. Forest fires in national forests were reduced by nearly half after the CCC began functioning as a firefighting unit. Apparently many fires had been deliberately set by men hoping to earn government money by helping to put them out.

The CCC men also surveyed and graded a number of new roads in the area, built bridges where needed, put gravel on existing roads, dug firebreaks and built dams for two new lakes—Lake Winfield Scott and Lake Trahlyta at Vogel State Park.

"The Army was responsible for us while we were in camp and we mustered just like regular recruits," the late Parley Kanaday related. "Once we went out on the job, we worked for and with the Forest Service, which provided us with picks and shovels and whatever other equipment we needed. I weighed only 120 pounds at the time, and after swinging a 19-lb. hammer all day crushing rock, I knew what it meant to be tired!"

The CCC was abolished in 1942 after the United States entered World War II and all able-bodied young men were needed in the armed forces. Parley Kanaday served in the navy and used money provided by the GI Bill to attend barber school when the war was over.

## LEARNING BY DOING AT WAHSEGA 4-H CENTER

After the CCC's Camp F-11 was closed, a camp for underprivileged children was established on the site in 1938. In the mid-'40s it became a 4-H Center that offered a summer camping program for 4-H Club members from all over the state.

The crude temporary CCC barracks were torn down and rustic cabins were built to blend in with the original stick-frame dining hall remaining from the CCC camp. Bill Casteel, a World War I veteran who had been stationed at Camp F-11, returned in 1946 to be resident manager. Since electricity was not available at the time, kerosene lamps used in the cabins had to be cleaned and refilled weekly. Bill's wife Effie and her staff did all the cooking on large coal stoves, and ice was brought in daily and stored in big iceboxes to provide refrigeration. Water from the mountain stream flowing through the camp was diverted by flume to create a small lake where campers could swim.

Every summer for over sixty years, two hundred 4-H Club campers have arrived at the Wahsega 4-H Center every Monday afternoon from early June through late July. After being greeted by a staff of counselors and assigned to their cabins, the campers are divided into family groups, and a lot of friendly competition goes on all week among the Hatfields and the McCoys, the Clampetts and the McDougals. While the other team names are derived from popular culture, the name McDougal comes from former residents in the Dahlonega area.

The next three days are spent in activities that today include forest and stream ecology, herpetology (learning about reptiles and amphibians), low ropes, ultimate frisbee, a 25-foot climbing wall, a 35-foot-high "dangle duo" or giant ladder, tubing on the Chestatee River and swimming. The zipline, a 3,005-foot wire strung from a tall pole to a lower one and often referred to in army training as the "slide for life," is another favorite outdoor activity.

While baseball was a popular pastime in previous years, free time today is characterized by the continuous bouncing of basketballs on the outdoor courts. In the evenings, campers and counselors all gather in the Rec Hall for dancing and special programs, including a talent show. Campers love dressing up for the costume contest, especially when the theme is space aliens.

In addition to participating in all the fun and games, each camper serves on KP duty. This usually involves assisting in the dining hall at mealtimes. Many young boys and girls have learned to sweep and mop while doing KP at Wahsega.

Before the campers leave for home on Friday morning, the group that has scored the most points during the week's activities is awarded the coveted "pot of gold."

In addition to the Cloverleaf summer program for fifth and sixth graders, Wahsega 4-H Center offers a Wilderness Challenge Camp for seventh and eighth graders that includes cave crawling and white-water rafting. There is also a one-week camp for 4-H students in high school. A new program called Operation 4-H: Joint Forces at the Falls was introduced in 2005. It is designed primarily for the children of military reservists on active duty, but it is also open to any youngster with a parent in any branch of the military.

Along with the other four 4-H centers in the state, Wahsega 4-H Center hosts the Georgia 4-H Environmental Education Program. It typically runs Monday through Wednesday and Wednesday through Friday for ten weeks in the spring and ten weeks in the fall. Designed for all school children in third through eighth grades, these programs are so educational that students attending are counted as being in school. The seasonal

Environmental Education instructors are college graduates hired from all over the nation to come teach these students.

The purpose of all that goes on at Wahsega 4-H Center is to challenge youngsters mentally and physically and help them develop a strong sense of responsibility for the environment as well as their own behavior. They gain confidence in their own ability as they learn by doing—and have lots of fun in the process.

## WORLD WAR II'S IMPACT ON DAHLONEGA'S HOLLY THEATRE

Many of Lumpkin County's sons and daughters joined military units and were sent across the oceans to serve their country during World War II. Back home, their families dealt with anxiety about relatives in harm's way and rationing of items like gasoline, meat and sugar. Letters written from loved ones near military fronts sometimes arrived with words cut out by censors looking for any information that might be detrimental to the security of the United States.

Movies shown at Dahlonega's Holly Theatre were preceded by *The Eyes and Ears of the World* newsreels starring Edward R. Murrow, relating war news and showing American troops in action around the world. During the war years the Holly's aging equipment frequently broke down, and owner Randall Holly Brannon had great difficulty getting replacement parts. He made an appeal to the war production board describing the breakdowns, stating, "We are experiencing a great deal of difficulty in getting the necessary replacement parts due to the fact that this equipment is obsolete."

When asked how the product requested would help the war effort or essential civilian needs, Brannon explained, "Motion picture theatres are cooperating wholeheartedly with the government in running salvage matinees, acting as salvage deposits, participating in the direct sales of war bonds and stamps and showing O.W.I. government film to stimulate the war effort." He also noted, "Equipment to be used in motion picture theatre which is the only house located in Dahlonega, Georgia, furnishing entertainment and keeping up morale for civilian community as well as U.S. Army Training Center or School."

The army training center Brannon referred to was the Army Specialized Training Reserve Program (ASTRP), which allowed seventeen-year-old males to participate in intense military training while attending college before being drafted when they reached the age of eighteen. These young men came from all over the United States to participate in the ASTRP program at North Georgia College before going off to war.

As World War II drew to an end, Brannon began making plans to erect a new theater. The building on the square currently in use was not only inadequate in size but also in such poor condition that he was concerned about his patrons' safety.

Even after the war was over, however, things did not soon return to normal. When Brannon applied for the needed building permit in September of 1946, it was denied. After being assured from several reliable sources that the Civilian Production Administration (CPA) in Washington would expire on March 31, 1947, Brannon broke ground on his new

After many delays in construction due to wartime shortages and regulations, Dahlonega's new Holly Theatre held its grand opening on July 12, 1948. *Courtesy of the Holly Theatre.*

site located on West Main Street at the beginning of the month, confident that government restrictions were ending.

What Brannon could not foresee was that at the last minute the CPA was transferred to another governmental department. The result was that construction and repairs throughout the United States continued to be restricted in order to utilize all available materials and labor to provide housing for returning war veterans. Controls on amusements were extended through February of the following year. Brannon received a disheartening telegram in May of 1947, ordering him to halt all construction immediately.

Numerous letters were written by many prominent Dahlonega citizens in Brannon's behalf, and Brannon himself made a special trip to Washington to plead his case in person, all to no avail. The needed permit was again denied, and the construction materials continued to deteriorate on the building site.

Finally, on December 23, 1947, Brannon received a telegram saying that the application had been approved and the permit granted. The building was soon completed, and the new Holly Theatre celebrated its grand opening to a capacity crowd of excited moviegoers on July 12, 1948.

## DUGAS'S RICH STRIKE AT THE CALHOUN MINE

A newsreel shown at the Holly and other theaters across the nation in November 1939 took time off from reporting Nazi aggression in Europe to show scenes from Dahlonega's Calhoun Mine, where a prospector named Graham Dugas had recently made a big strike. The story was also featured prominently in the *New York Times* and other newspapers with such sensational headlines as, "Rich vein is found in century old Dahlonega Mine" and "Rich vein opening at the Calhoun mine assays up to $75,000 a ton." Some predicted that Dugas's find would rival the big strikes made in California back in 1849.

State Geologist Garland Peyton was quoted as saying, "Frankly, I am impressed with what I have seen, but there is no way of telling how far down it goes until the rock has been blasted." Dugas, however, was apparently in no hurry to do any blasting—except for the time he was showing his operation to some movie scouts. The detonation he set off then with their cameras running was reported to have revealed a new vein of gold. Dugas enjoyed all the publicity and sent press releases with photographs to newspapers that had not previously carried the story. He also let it be known that there were a few shares of stock in the mine that just might be available for purchase.

Dugas's automobile contributed to his fame almost as much as his strike at the Calhoun Mine. People frequently didn't remember the make of the vehicle, but they never tired of describing how its metal parts were plated with gold taken from the mine.

There's no doubt that Graham Dugas hit a rich pocket of gold, but apparently the vein quickly played out without forming any more pockets. A final headline announced that creditors had attached the mining equipment at the Calhoun to satisfy claims against Dugas. There was no mention of what became of his famed gold-plated auto.

## THE POULTRY INDUSTRY COMES TO LUMPKIN COUNTY

In 1930 Jesse Jewell began managing his family's feed business in Gainesville, Georgia. Business was slow due to the economic depression, so he decided to try a new approach in the hopes of boosting feed sales. He purchased a number of baby chicks and made them available—along with feed—on credit to farmers lacking available cash. When the chickens were grown, Jewell bought them back at a price that enabled farmers to turn a profit after reimbursing him for the baby chicks and feed.

Soon many farmers in Hall and neighboring counties, including Lumpkin, were raising baby chickens on contract with Jewell. The state of Georgia was not among the ten largest broiler-producing states prior to 1940, but by 1945 it had moved into third place with 29,520 chickens. Georgia had moved into second place by 1950 and first place by 1955, where it remained through 1970, when the state raised 453,886 broilers.

Prior to 1930 most people kept a few chickens to provide eggs and an occasional meal. Most chickens were not confined because many local folks thought it was natural for chickens to run loose and roost in trees. Besides, free-range chickens subsisted on bugs and whatever else they could find to eat, so they didn't have to be fed. However, when folks began to discover that hens kept in houses continued to lay eggs all winter, it wasn't long before every farm had its chicken house.

About the time Jesse Jewell was starting his contract chicken business in Gainesville, a Dahlonega shoe repairman named Alec Housley speculated that raising chickens could be a way to improve the lives of Lumpkin County farmers so they wouldn't have to be at the mercy of the weather. He built a small chicken house in back of his house and acquired 350 chicks, which he protected from disease the newfangled way—by inoculating the mother hens. He was so successful that he eventually expanded his capacity to 10,000.

William Gladstone Owens arrived in Dahlonega in 1929 as Lumpkin County's first county agent, and he helped local farmers improve their methods of growing chickens as well as crops. In the late '30s he built a model two-story chicken house and filled it with 3,500 layers. In 1946 he put incubators in the building and switched to producing chicks for the broiler industry.

Following Owens's premature death in 1954 at age fifty-seven, his son Erwin moved back to Dahlonega to take over the business and was joined a couple of years later by his brother Bill. They opened the first feed mill in Dahlonega and processed eggs for shipment to markets in New York. They built a new hatchery in 1970, which they sold to Tyson in 1986.

Lee Anderson, another pioneer in the poultry industry, started out growing chickens for Jesse Jewell and Martin Feed and Poultry. There weren't many hatcheries in Georgia at the time, so he imported some chicks from out of state. Lee and his son Marvin later became partners with Tom T. Folger in building and operating the Dahlonega Hatchery, which was housed in three brick buildings on Highway 19. Over the years they increased their capacity from 60,000 chicks a week to 200,000 in 1955. The three partners also owned another company called Dahlonega Feed & Poultry.

Within a decade Lumpkin County farmers went from keeping a few yard chickens that weighed less than three pounds each to raising 100,000 chickens that would grow to four pounds in six to eight weeks. The poultry industry not only brought more prosperity to an area that was chronically economically depressed, it also improved the water quality by requiring less land to be plowed and cultivated, thereby reducing the amount of soil erosion into the streams. Litter from the chicken houses enriched the soil without need for commercial fertilizers.

The poultry industry is still active in Lumpkin County, but today most chickens are raised by independent growers who have contracts with large processing companies.

9

# Dahlonega since 1950: History Still in the Making

## RANGERS TRAIN AT CAMP FRANK D. MERRILL

The history of the American Ranger is a long and colorful saga of courage, daring and outstanding leadership. Ranger missions were primarily defensive until 1675, when a company of independent Rangers from Plymouth Colony proved successful in raiding hostile Indians during King Phillip's War.

In 1756 Major Robert Rogers of New Hampshire recruited nine companies of American frontiersmen that became the first permanently organized Rangers. They wore distinctive green outfits and developed tactics called "Standing Orders Rogers Rules," which the British of that day considered unconventional but are still in use by Rangers today. Since then, Rangers have distinguished themselves by their valor in many trouble spots around the world, including Vietnam and Iraq.

Rangers first came to Lumpkin County for mountain training in 1950 and moved to their present location eleven miles north of town in 1959. The Mountain Ranger Camp was designated Camp Frank D. Merrill in honor of the general who led the first American unit to confront the Japanese army on Asian soil during World War II. In the summer of 1943, President Roosevelt asked for three thousand volunteers to train for a special mission to infiltrate behind Japanese lines in Burma. All were required to be in a "high state of physical ruggedness and stamina" for this "extremely hazardous mission." General Frank D. Merrill commanded these tough jungle fighters, who earned the nickname Merrill's Marauders.

The mission of the Fifth Ranger Training Battalion at Camp Merrill is to train leaders under conditions similar to those found in combat. The mountain phase they experience in north Georgia is the second of three Ranger training phases. Their mountaineer training includes rappelling, patrolling, small unit tactics, raids and ambushes.

Camp Merrill holds an annual Mountain Ranger Run and open house in mid-May. The day begins with races ranging from a one-mile fun run to a strenuous fifteen-kilometer Ranger run. All proceeds from entrance fees benefit local charities.

An army Ranger practices rappelling as part of his mountaineering training. *Copyright Greg Janney/All You Need Photography.*

During the open house that follows, the public is invited to watch Rangers show what it takes to do their jobs. Visitors are given the opportunity to personally experience some Ranger activities, such as looking through night vision goggles, firing a machine gun (with blanks) and climbing a rock wall.

Rangers demonstrate their skills in free-fall parachute jumping, rappelling, dropping out of helicopters and mountain rescue. The Fifth Army Rangers have often assisted in real life search and rescue operations in the Chattahoochee National Forest, in which they have located lost hikers and saved lives.

## INDUSTRIES COME TO DAHLONEGA

### *Lees Carpets and Mohawk Industries*

In 1955 earthmoving equipment began grading a hilltop east of Dahlonega to create a large level area. The news that Lees Carpets was going to build a plant on the site to make yarn for carpets was soon the talk of the town. The local economy had been boosted by the poultry industry but jobs were still scarce.

When the Pine Tree Plant was completed, Lees Carpets had no trouble finding employees. J.L. Eastwick, president of the company, noted that he found the mountain people he employed to be very "resourceful, independent, cooperative, and loyal."

Lees Carpets merged with Burlington Industries and took the Burlington name in 1960, but production went on as usual until the early '70s, when the plant converted from making woolen yarn to nylon in order to meet market and style demands. This process involved changing or adapting a large part of the equipment.

The name of the plant was changed again in 1998 when Mohawk Industries bought the facility from Burlington and upgraded the operation. Today Mohawk employs 370 people in its operation of manufacturing yarn for carpets.

### *Southern Switches*

Southern Switches began operations in Lumpkin County in 1965 with six employees in a small rented building on the Public Square. The first part of the ten-thousand-square-foot plant on Happy Hollow Road was completed in 1967. Since then five additions have been made to the building.

Southern Switches is a division of INDAK, which had its beginning as a family-owned toy business in Northbrook, Illinois. During the 1940s it expanded its production to include switches for refrigerators, washing machines and other appliances. As the company continued to grow, it began making switches for automobiles and tractors and opened subsidiary plants in Georgia at Clarkesville, Cleveland and Dahlonega.

Danny Goss, who was plant manager of Southern Switches for thirty-two years, recalls shipping three hundred thousand switches a week during peak times. The company ships directly to all the main automotive, lawn mower and tractor companies in the United States.

## *Torrington–Timken*

The Torrington Company purchased sixty-eight acres of land in Lumpkin County and broke ground in April of 1979. While the plant was under construction, the company hired employees and trained them in the old school bus maintenance shop. After the 148,000-square-foot building was completed, Torrington's Dahlonega plant opened its doors with a ribbon-cutting ceremony held July 22, 1980.

The first order of automotive roller bearings shipped the following October totaled 3.3 million pieces and was a typical month's supply utilized by Ford, Chrysler and General Motors. The plant's output doubled over the next decade. The Torrington plant quickly grew to be a high-volume producer of pins, rollers and planet shafts, supplying the major automotive companies as well as sister Torrington plants. Most new vehicles on the road today have some Dahlonega product in their transmissions or engines.

In 2003 the Torrington Company was purchased from Ingersoll-Rand by Timken Bearings. In his letter entitled "The Silver Anniversary in the City of Gold" published in the September 2005 issue of *Timken*, Human Resource Manager Roger Yonts related that Dahlonega was chosen as the location for the Torrington plant because of two things: "First, the work ethic of the people in the Dahlonega area; and second, the support demonstrated by the community at large for the new facility." He also noted that the Dahlonega plant was named the "Center of Excellence" for roller manufacturing.

Timken-Dahlonega today has 250 employees, including many who have worked at the plant ever since Torrington began operations in 1980. Timken announced plans in 2005 to expand production at the Dahlonega plant and is planning to grow to 300 people by 2007.

# DAHLONEGA BUILDS A HOSPITAL

Although Dahlonega acquired a small medical clinic in 1939, serious illnesses and trauma required a sometimes life-threatening trip to the hospital in Gainesville, twenty miles away. In the early 1970s, the chamber of commerce began to discuss the possibility of building a local hospital. A ten-member Hospital Authority was created in March of 1973 by Lumpkin County Commissioner J.B. Jones.

After visiting hospitals in cities comparable in size to Dahlonega, the Lumpkin County Hospital Authority selected an architect and made the decision to sell revenue bonds as the means for constructing and equipping the local facility. This means of financing meant that Lumpkin County residents would not bear the cost of the building for at least two years, by which time it was hoped that the hospital would pay for itself.

Enthusiasm about the prospect of having a local hospital motivated a strong spirit of cooperation within the community. Land on Crown Mountain was donated for a site and when it proved to be too small, tracts of surrounding land were also contributed to the cause. Families and churches donated rooms for the eagerly anticipated hospital.

Six months after the Authority was created, ground was broken for the new hospital and work began immediately to clear and excavate the 16.5 acres of land where it was to be situated. To avoid the common problem of insufficient space for future expansion, the architectural design called for an additional top floor, which would be left vacant until needed.

Getting water to the top of Crown Mountain for the facility proved to be a problem, as the city did not have a reservoir that high, but it was solved by building the hospital's own water tower. Finding doctors willing to come to Dahlonega to staff the hospital also required some recruiting but was eventually accomplished. Dahlonega's very own hospital opened its doors on June 1, 1976. Rangers from Camp Merrill used their rope-climbing skills to place the medical symbol on the front of the newly completed building.

Originally called Lumpkin County Hospital, the facility was purchased from the county during the '80s by St. Joseph's Hospital and run by the Sisters of Mercy for several years. Money from the sale was put into an Indigent Care Fund.

Chestatee Regional Hospital was purchased in 2000 by SunLink Health Systems. Today it is an accredited full-service forty-nine-bed facility that offers quality healthcare with a warm hometown approach and a therapeutic view of the beautiful north Georgia mountains. In 2006 Chestatee Regional was named as a recipient of Solucient's 100 Top Hospitals Performance Improvement Leaders Award. It was one of only twenty rural hospitals nationwide to achieve this honor.

## DAHLONEGA GOLD FOR THE CAPITOL DOME WAS CARRIED BY WAGON TRAIN

It is said that you can take a person out of Dahlonega, but you can't take Dahlonega out of a person. As former Dahlonega resident Gordon Price sat in his Atlanta law office looking out at the state capitol, he visualized how the dome would look covered with Dahlonega gold.

Price took his idea to capitol architect A. Thomas Bradbury and the two of them presented their plan to Secretary of State Ben W. Fortson Jr. and Governor Marvin Griffin. When the governor was assured that gold for the project would be donated, he also became enthusiastic.

The Dahlonega Chamber of Commerce headed the quest for the precious metal. Citizens of town and county prospected for any grain or fleck that had been overlooked by miners in the past. Descendants of miners donated gold that had been in their family for years and people without gold gave money for its purchase. The necessary forty-three ounces was collected in just three months.

It would have been much easier and safer to ship the gold to Atlanta by armored car. However, local historian Madeleine Anthony thought it would be more newsworthy to carry the gold to the capitol by wagon train. Despite dire predictions about the difficulties and dangers of such an outmoded means of travel in 1958, the idea began to catch on. Numbers of people began rounding up mules and wagons and old-fashioned attire typical of the 1800s.

On the morning of August 4, 1958, seven wagons loaded with passengers ranging in age from four to sixty circled the courthouse and headed down the highway to Atlanta. The two state patrol cars assigned to escort them had to drop out because they couldn't keep their batteries charged at the plodding rate of three miles per hour. It therefore fell to wagon master Hughes Moore and scout Billy Moore to ride their horses at the front and rear of

In 1958 Dahlonega gold destined for the capitol dome was carried to Atlanta by an old-time wagon train. *Courtesy of the Lumpkin County Library.*

the wagon train carrying red flags. Since the highway at that time had only two lanes, it was their job to stop all traffic and route it single file around the wagons.

All along the way people gathered to watch the wagon train pass. Many offered the travelers watermelon and soft drinks to quench their thirst in the summer heat. The first night was spent in the town of Cumming, where men, women and children slept in or on the ground under their wagons. The people of Alpharetta served lunch for the travelers on the second day of their journey and the mayor of Roswell gave them the key to the city when they arrived in the evening. The people of Roswell not only provided supper but also opened the town's swimming pool to them.

Excitement was high the next day as the wagon train headed down Peachtree Street toward the capitol with police cars as escorts and the Third Army Band playing patriotic music. Scout Billy Moore rode his horse Flash up the capitol steps, firing his muzzleloader (loaded with paper) and yelling, "Where's the governor? The gold is here!"

Madeleine Anthony and Louella Moore, dressed in old-fashioned dresses and sun bonnets, carried the precious cargo in an old chest that once belonged to William Few—one of Georgia's 1787 signers of the United States Constitution—on loan from the State Department of Archives for the occasion.

Madeleine Anthony and Louella Moore are shown carrying gold for the capitol dome in an old chest that once belonged to William Few, one of Georgia's 1787 signers of the U.S. Constitution. *Courtesy of the Lumpkin County Library.*

Governor Griffin appeared and accepted the gift of gold formally presented by Bill Fry, president of the Dahlonega Chamber of Commerce. The governor expressed his appreciation to the people of Lumpkin County, saying, "The colorful journey to deliver this gold in a proper historical manner will certainly illustrate not only the native pride of Georgians in their historical heritage but should bring this event into national focus."

The forty-three ounces of gold were sent to Philadelphia to be converted into gold leaf one-five-thousandth of an inch thick. The three-hundred-foot rolls were sent back to Atlanta and applied to the capitol dome by steeplejacks. After its gilding with Dahlonega gold, the dome became an even more prominent Atlanta landmark.

## GOLD FROM LOCAL MINES GILDED THE COLLEGE STEEPLE

After Dahlonega gold was taken to Atlanta to gild the capitol dome, some local people began talking about how nice the North Georgia College steeple would look if gold leaf could be applied to it as well. R.D. Hogue heard about the project and offered to donate eleven ounces of gold he had previously mined at the Josephine Mine, which he purchased in 1950. Two additional ounces required for the gilding were donated by the Crisson Mine and the local chamber of commerce.

Funds needed to have the gold leaf applied to the forty-foot-high steeple of Price Memorial Hall were raised by the Dahlonega Club, with almost four hundred donors contributing. When the gold had been refined and milled into tissue-thin strips, steeplejacks put them into place in time for the college's centennial celebration in 1973. Since then the sight of the golden steeple gleaming in the sunlight immediately draws attention as one approaches the town from any direction.

## THE TUGBOAT USS *DAHLONEGA*

A delegation of folks from Dahlonega including the mayor traveled to Norfolk, Virginia, in 1964 to attend the commissioning of a U.S. Navy tugboat named the USS *Dahlonega.* Personnel at the naval station were surprised by the number of enthusiastic Dahlonegans who showed up to see "their tugboat."

Apparently no other community sent a delegation, even though all navy yard tugs of the same class were given titles of towns with Native American names. Three television stations covered the commissioning ceremony and a Norfolk newspaper printed the story with a two-column picture, whereas the launching of an atomic submarine the next day rated only a couple of inches!

Following the ceremony, the delegation from Dahlonega was taken on an hour-and-a-half cruise and served lunch in the tug's mess hall. They learned that the tugboat's mission would be primarily to move aircraft carriers and other large vessels in and out of the harbor.

Mayor Garner was later quoted as saying, "We didn't get to hear about the tug much because the crew members wouldn't stop asking us questions about the town the boat was

*Above:* The USS *Dahlonega* displayed her firefighting equipment to visitors from Dahlonega who traveled to Naval Station Norfolk to see their tugboat. *Courtesy of Naval Station Norfolk.*

*Opposite:* R.D. Hogue, owner of the Josephine Mine, donated eleven of the thirteen ounces needed to gild the college steeple in 1973. *Courtesy of the author.*

named for." They had no previous knowledge where Dahlonega was located or what the name meant.

In 1996, another delegation from Dahlonega—including four members of the original party—gathered at Naval Station Norfolk to celebrate the tugboat's thirty-two years of "dedicated service to the fleet." The ship's railings were decorated with red, white and blue bunting, and all of her surfaces appeared freshly scrubbed or painted. The naval station's commanding officer noted that the day was about "pride and commitment," not only on the part of the tug's crew but also the people of Dahlonega who cared enough to come see their tugboat.

Following the ceremony, the visitors from Dahlonega were invited to come aboard the tugboat for a tour of the harbor. The 2,200-horsepower engine was cranked up and crewmembers who had been in dress uniforms earlier appeared at their stations in work clothes. Seaman Felicia Jennings skillfully loosened the heavy mooring rope and leapt gracefully from the dock to the moving tug.

After the USS *Dahlonega* returned to her mooring and all guests had disembarked, the tug again took to the water, this time to display her firefighting equipment. As great jets of water shot high into the air and splashed wetly over the decks, it was apparent why the display had not be done with guests still aboard! The tugboat bade them farewell with a musical medley of toots and whistles.

The USS *Dahlonega* has since been decommissioned and is no longer in use. The navy donated the tug's wheel to the people of Dahlonega, and it remains on display in the lobby of City Hall.

## GOLD RUSH DAYS AND OTHER EVENTS

Most towns have their own special festivals today, but when Dahlonega initiated its first Gold Rush Days celebration in 1954, it was an innovative event. The original purpose was to commemorate and promote the community's gold mining history by recreating it. Local people clad in old-fashioned clothing demonstrated everything from churning and spinning to splitting wooden shingles and making moonshine, described as "the art and science of turning corn on the cob into corn in the jug."

Men started weeks in advance growing beards for the occasion, while women sewed long dresses and old-time bonnets to wear in the fashion show featuring pioneer dress. Merchants decorated their storefronts with historical displays or rough board slabs to make them look like the gold rush town of the 1830s. Many organizations built floats depicting scenes from the early days of the community to enter in the parade.

As publicity went out describing the event, inquiries came from as far away as Maine and California. In addition to all the first-time visitors, many former residents returned to Dahlonega for the occasion, making it a gala homecoming. Attendance at the first Gold Rush Days celebration was estimated at five thousand people.

The festivities began at 10:00 a.m. when a man impersonating Benjamin Parks rode bareback into town, yelling that he had discovered gold. Wagons and buggies were on hand

Ross McDonald and Nina McClure Head were crowned King and Queen of Dahlonega's first Gold Rush Days celebration in 1954. Ross was a lifelong gold miner who owned numerous well-known mines. "Aunt Nine" was very active in community affairs, including the project of gilding the steeple of Price Memorial Hall.
*Courtesy of Helen Head Green.*

to convey people to the gold mine and museum at the foot of Crown Mountain to watch demonstrations of gold panning and to try it themselves.

A little later, the elegantly attired King and Queen of the Gold Rush were duly crowned and led the parade through the town. The first kings and queens were chosen because of their association with gold mining either as miners themselves or as descendants of miners.

In addition to people dressed as pioneers, gold miners and Indians, there were real Indians who came from Cherokee, North Carolina. After the parade they played a game of Cherokee stickball on the college athletic field. Other old-fashioned games and contests provided entertainment for both participants and spectators. These included a hog-calling contest and such challenging activities as attempting to catch a greased pig and climbing a greased fifteen-foot pole to claim the $5 prize on top. The day concluded with fiddlers playing for a lively square dance held on the streets of the Public Square.

Originally sponsored by the Dahlonega/Lumpkin County Chamber of Commerce and later by the Jaycees, the festival continued to grow in popularity and attendance. Well-known announcers from Atlanta television stations served as masters of ceremonies. More exhibits and displays were added along with events like arm wrestling, horseshoe-pitching, buck dancing, clogging and a lumberjack contest in which two men wielding a crosscut saw vied to cut through an eight-inch-thick log in the shortest amount of time.

Since its inception in 1954, Dahlonega's Gold Rush Days Festival has been held every year except 1967 and 1968 and is no longer the small local event it once was. Craftspeople and tradespeople now come from all over the Southeast to set up their tents and sell their wares, and crowds in excess of two hundred thousand people attend the celebration. The event is so popular that it is consistently selected as one of the "Top 20 Events in the Southeast" by the Southeast Tourism Society. It is held the third weekend in October.

## *Family Day and Independence Day Celebration*

Dahlonega's second longest-running festival is its annual Family and Independence Day Celebration, which began in 1976 as a commemoration of America's two hundredth birthday. Longtime resident Ella Ray Oakes initiated the event and has coordinated it annually for thirty years.

The opening ceremony is appropriately patriotic as the NGCSU Color Guard, military personnel from the Ranger Camp and local Boy Scouts participate in the presentation of the colors, raising of the flag and recitation of the Pledge of Allegiance. Following a reading of the Preamble to the Constitution of the United States, local soloists sing the national anthem, "Proud to Be an American" and "God Bless America" before the keynote speaker delivers remarks appropriate to the occasion.

Special events taking place throughout the day include gold panning, pony rides, bingo games, watermelon cutting and various musical performances. There are also demonstrations of pioneer skills such as quilting, weaving and chair caning. Booths offer food, crafts and other gift items. The day concludes with a dazzling fireworks display at the college drill field.

Dahlonega's Fourth of July celebration has frequently been selected as one of the "Top 20 Events in the Southeast" and has been featured in several national magazines, including *Southern Living* and the *National Profile.*

## *Bear on the Square Festival*

Dahlonega's Bear on the Square Festival was started in 1997 to commemorate a unique event in the town's history. The previous May, a mother bear and yearling cub wandered into town and were frightened by the sight of humans strolling around the Public Square. Mama Bear fled for the hills, while Baby Bear took refuge in a tall sycamore tree and lodged himself in the fork of a branch.

As people gathered to gape at the terrified bear cub, Sheriff Berry arrived and quickly cordoned off the area around the tree. He then sent a deputy to bring blankets to use as a net. When Wildlife Ranger Chuck Waters appeared on the scene with a tranquilizer dart gun, the crowd fell silent, watching to see what would happen. As the dart penetrated its thigh, the little bear squealed in alarm and scrambled higher into the tree, but moments later, it began to lose consciousness. As the little creature began to fall, the crowd held its collective breath, and the sheriff and a number of volunteers tightened their grip on the blankets. When the cub landed safely in the improvised net, simultaneous clapping and cheering broke out among the onlookers.

The seventy-pound young bear was ear-tagged and released into the Chattahoochee Wildlife Management Area, but his misadventure into the Dahlonega Public Square was the talk of the town for weeks. After local musicians Nick and Glenda Pender wrote a song about the event, several merchants conceived the idea of a Bear on the Square Festival that would feature bluegrass and old-time music along with authentic Appalachian crafts.

Held the third weekend in April, this festival offers various musical workshops and concerts presented by well-known performers. Spontaneous jam sessions occur all around the Public Square as groups of musicians improvise together on old-time fiddle tunes, Appalachian ballads and early country and bluegrass tunes. An old-time mountain dance takes place on Saturday evenings. Children's activities include a Teddy Bear's Picnic and an interactive play entitled *Goldlocks and the Three Bears on the Square*, in which audience members become actors on stage or supply sound effects.

In just two years, Dahlonega's Bear on the Square Festival became so popular that in 1999 the *Atlanta Journal-Constitution* named it one of the "Top 10 Spring Festivals in the Southeast." In 2006 the American Business Association designated it as one of "America's Top 100 Festivals."

Bear on the Square continues to grow annually as more and more people discover how much fun it is to wander around the historic Dahlonega Public Square, listening to musicians play foot-tapping tunes, watching skilled artisans demonstrate their traditional crafts and hearing the story of how a little bear wandered into town one day and started the whole thing.

## *Mountain Flower Art Festival and Garden Expo*

This festival, held the third weekend in May, celebrates both mountain wildflowers and the craftspeople of northeast Georgia. All arts and crafts submissions are evaluated for originality and quality of craftsmanship by the artist.

A yearling bear cub wandered into the Public Square in the spring of 1996 and climbed into a tall sycamore tree. The event inspired a song, which led to a musical festival called Bear on the Square. *Courtesy of Terry Rosso.*

The festival includes an annual spring Garden Expo presented by the Georgia Mountains Master Gardeners. Programs and demonstrations by these Master Gardeners offer advice on topics such as growing native plants, seed starting, container gardening, making trough gardens and dealing with problem plants. The Garden Expo also features wildflower displays and walks, a demonstration garden of native plants, children's activities and a large plant and seed sale.

The festival is presented by the Dahlonega Merchants' Association and sponsored by the Dahlonega Arts Council and Lumpkin County Bank. It is held at Hancock Park, located two blocks from the Public Square on the corner of North Park and Hawkins Streets.

### *Autumn Fest*

Autumn Fest is held the third weekend in September and sets the mood for the beginning of the autumn season. The Public Square is colorfully decorated with corn stalks, pumpkins, bales of hay and Indian corn. This festival is sponsored by the Dahlonega Merchants' Association and originally began as a sidewalk sale. Today booths are set up around the square, and merchants hold sales inside their stores.

### *Old Fashioned Christmas*

Unlike most of Dahlonega's other festivals, which are held on third weekends, Old Fashioned Christmas begins the first weekend in December and lasts until December 25. Santa Claus arrives just in time for the Christmas parade at 5:00 p.m. on the first Saturday. Following the parade, caroling takes place around the Public Square until the Tree Lighting Ceremony at 7:00 p.m. When the switch is thrown, Dahlonega's historic Public Square takes on the appearance of a magical fairyland as thousands of tiny white lights are turned on, outlining buildings and trees. Shops stay open late, and many merchants offer hot cider and cookies to visitors.

Other events offered during Old Fashioned Christmas vary from year to year but usually include a Festival of Trees & Wreaths, open house at the historic Vickery House and a tour of other historic homes and local inns. The Lumpkin County Library offers "Fireside Stories and Music" for the whole family. Live reindeer and the world-famous Clydesdale horses are often popular attractions. Children can find Santa Claus in front of the Welcome Center on weekends and can have their pictures taken sitting with him in his sleigh.

### *Literary Festival*

Dahlonega's newest festival was founded in 2004 by Kate Quigley McElliott and NGCSU professor Brian Jay Corrigan in order to promote literary awareness and establish a network of communication among writers. The schedule of events includes workshops and seminars, storytelling, book signings and keynote speakers. Seminars are conducted by published writers and topics range from how to do research to advice on getting published. The festival also sponsors contests for short stories and novels and offers children's events.

The Dahlonega Literary Festival is described as "a celebration of the written word." It is held in February on Presidents' Day weekend, beginning on Friday evening and running through Sunday.

## *World Gold Panning Championships*

Gold panning enthusiasts come from far and wide to observe and participate in the World Gold Panning Championships held annually in Dahlonega the third weekend in April. This is the only panning contest of its kind to be recognized in the *Guinness Book of World Records*. Originally founded in 1961 to commemorate the 1842 discovery of gold in southern California, the event has been held at the Consolidated Gold Mines of Dahlonega since 1992.

Contestants are given a ten-inch miner's pan filled with sand. Buried in the sand are eight small gold nuggets, which must be recovered by removing all other materials through the panning process. The same pan and gold nuggets have been used over the years to ensure consistency and fairness. The contestant who accomplishes the task in the shortest amount of time wins the championship.

The contest offers several divisions in both the State and World Championships, including youth, seniors, men, women and open. Every year an inductee into the Gold Panner's Hall of Fame is announced and recognized for his or her contributions to the advancement of gold panning as an art, a pastime and a spectator sport.

## *Cycling Events*

The steep and winding roads in Lumpkin County attract many bicycle enthusiasts who come to test their wheels, leg muscles and stamina on the steep but scenic grades.

Dahlonega is the Stage Four Finish for the Tour de Georgia, and many cycling fans line the streets to watch the bicycles come flying into town. This is a six-day, six-stage race that covers more than six hundred miles, much of it through mountainous terrain. It is North America's only Hors Classe (2.HC) professional cycling stage race and draws the most elite cyclists. Proceeds from the race benefit the Georgia Cancer Coalition. The bicyclers traditionally arrive in Dahlonega around mid-afternoon on the fourth Friday in April.

Thousands of people flocked to Dahlonega in 2005 to see Lance Armstrong ride. After winning the Tour de Georgia, this legendary cyclist went on to win the Tour de France for the seventh consecutive time before retiring from professional racing. While he was in Dahlonega, he was presented with a "face jug" made by local potter Brad Walker.

In September the Dahlonega/Lumpkin County Chamber of Commerce hosts the Six Gap Century and Three Gap Fifty Bike Ride, which draws thousands of cyclists from around the country and is the largest cycling event of its kind in the Southeast.

# THE GOLDEN MILLENNIUM CELEBRATION

The New Year and the New Millennium were royally welcomed in Dahlonega in ways that commemorated the community's past while creating new history in the process. The project was planned and implemented through the vision and leadership of Jean Cuthbertson and sponsored by the Dahlonega Women's Club. Funds were raised by selling a Golden Millennium 2000 Celebration medal struck to commemorate the occasion.

The celebration began at 2:00 p.m. on December 31, 1999, with the dedication of a Millennium Garden behind the Lumpkin County Library. The crowd moved to the Lumpkin County Courthouse at 2:30 for the unveiling of a mural of the Dahlonega Public Square, presented as a gift to the county by the Dahlonega/Lumpkin County Art Alliance. The ceremony also included the unveiling and dedication of seven medallions depicting scenes from local history, painted on the walls of the courthouse by members of the Art Alliance.

At 3:00 p.m. two life-sized bronze statues were unveiled and dedicated in front of the courthouse. The figure of a Cherokee pays tribute to Lumpkin County's Native American heritage, and a miner with a shovel and gold pan represents the county's gold-mining history. Both statues were commissioned for the Golden Millennium celebration and were created by Gainesville sculptor Gregory Johnson.

An impressive twenty-nine-foot tree-shaped piece of art cut from plate steel was dedicated at 4:00 p.m. in the city park. This History Tree depicts local history in seven tiers beginning with prehistoric wildlife at the bottom. Native Americans, early settlers, gold mining, the 1836 courthouse, the Dahlonega Branch Mint, North Georgia College and the Public Square today are portrayed successively on the upper tiers. The date 2000 crowns the top of the pole. The work was created by Steve O'Rear and Harriett DeWitt.

At 10:15 p.m. a large crowd gathered in front of the Welcome Center on the Public Square to take part in a Peace Vigil led by the Dahlonega Ministerial Association. Participants lit candles and lifted their voices to sing "Let There Be Peace on Earth." All then read a "Litany of Peace" attributed to Mother Teresa. Several prominent citizens spoke on the topic "What Peace Means to Me." A community choir premiered a work entitled "Crossroads," composed for the Millennium celebration by Dr. Joe Chapman and directed by Dr. Jack Broman, both members of the music faculty at NGCSU.

At the stroke of midnight, a golden nugget was dropped from the flagpole in front of the Welcome Center to the traditional strains of "Auld Lang Syne," as 1999 was ushered out and the year 2000 and the new millennium were welcomed in.

## DAHLONEGA'S SPIRIT OF PATRIOTISM

Dahlonega is noted for its spirit of patriotism, which has been expressed in rallies for support of troops and the creation of a veteran's park. This spirit of American pride is particularly apparent on holidays such as Memorial Day, the Fourth of July and Veterans Day. A week or so ahead of time, volunteers can be seen putting up flags and markers honoring deceased veterans around the Public Square and on all major roads coming into town.

The project began in 2000 when Jack Smoot suggested it to the Blue Mountain Masonic Lodge No. 38, where other members soon caught his enthusiasm. The first step was seeking permission from the city council, the county commissioner and the department of transportation to place the memorial markers on the roadsides. The next step was obtaining names of deceased veterans from the probate judge's office and creating the markers. Congressman Nathan Deal agreed to provide flags at cost.

Moved by the sight of flags waving over the names of men who served their country in the armed forces, many people began submitting names of their own. By 2005 the number

This life-sized bronze statue of a gold miner was commissioned for Dahlonega's Golden Millennium celebration as a symbol of the area's gold-mining history. *Courtesy of the author.*

Flags and markers honoring deceased veterans are placed around the Public Square and on all major roads coming into Dahlonega during the week of patriotic holidays. *Courtesy of the author.*

of markers had grown from 28 to 355, with new applications still being processed. Seeing teams of volunteers putting up the markers, townspeople and visitors alike often stop to express their appreciation and sometimes donate money to assist with expenses. Visitors frequently report being inspired to start similar projects in their hometowns. For that reason, volunteers have put together an information kit telling how to get started.

There are no ranks before the names on the markers. Privates and generals alike are designated only by their names and the war they served in. Not all are from Lumpkin County, but the people who submit their names are required to be local citizens. The only other criterion is that the veteran must have been honorably discharged. Cost of a marker is $60 and forms are available at the Welcome Center.

With the number of markers rapidly approaching four hundred, many volunteers are needed to put them up and take them down, even though the teams now speed up the process by using electric hammers to drive the stakes into the ground. "We couldn't get all the markers up before time to take them down without lots of volunteers helping," says Andy Howard, who has been involved with the project from the beginning. "We're lucky in that lots of people see this as something to be proud of."

## ARTS AND ENTERTAINMENT IN DAHLONEGA

Approximately two million people visit Dahlonega annually. They come to learn about its history and enjoy the carefully preserved yesteryear atmosphere of the town's Public Square. Some have an interest in visiting a real gold mine and in trying their hands at panning for gold, but the majority of visitors today are drawn by three relatively new attractions: entertainment, art and wineries.

Since the historic Holly Theatre reopened in 1993 after two decades of near abandonment, Dahlonega has experienced an exponential increase in performance and visual arts venues. In 2005 the Holly Theatre entertained over three thousand people with movies and high quality live performances ranging from musicals to murder mysteries.

Ranked as one of the top seven entertainment venues in the state of Georgia, the Holly is home to an active theater company, which annually produces five main stage shows, three dinner theater shows and other special events. The children's theater presents two or three productions a year and offers after-school drama classes and summer camps.

The Crimson Moon, located in an original 1858 storehouse on the Public Square, is a popular acoustic venue that provides opportunities for up-and-coming musicians and songwriters, as well as entertainment for the public. To fulfill its mission "to support, promote, and reward creativity," the Crimson Moon hosts a wide variety of acoustic performers from all over the Southeast. The eclectic entertainment—ranging from old-time and bluegrass to contemporary folk and blues—is complemented by Chef Rick's creative cuisine.

Strings 'n Things Coffee House offers a once-a-month evening of music from many traditions and other performing arts, including dance, storytelling and juggling. It is held in the fellowship hall of Dahlonega United Methodist Church and is a joint project of the church and the Wiggins Group. Performances begin at 7:00 p.m. on the third Saturday of each month.

Since 2004 the Buisson Arts Center Gallery and Performance Hall has served as an incubator for the arts community by offering artists opportunities to express themselves in both visual and performing arts. It sponsors eighteen to twenty shows a year and features concerts that range from classical to bluegrass. The performance hall is the former sanctuary of the 1897 Dahlonega Baptist Church, and the fellowship hall has been converted to a gallery that is a showcase for regional artists. It is also the setting for dinner theaters and children's productions presented by the Holly Theatre Company. The Buisson Center offers ongoing classes in many mediums, including oil, watercolors, acrylic, drawing, ceramics, weaving, quilting and photography.

The Olde Cannery Arts Center is located in a historic building that was originally built by the WPA (Works Project Administration) in the late 1930s. After being used as a community cannery for a number of years, it became a popular thrift shop. It was renovated in 2003 by the Dahlonega Arts Council and is now a gallery housing various mediums of visual art by area artists. Recent exhibits have featured folk art, fiber arts, photography and various theme shows.

At the outside-the-box Bleu Art Gallery, artists can be seen at work, creating art live at their easels. In addition to its paintings, the gallery is known for its drawings, pottery, jewelry, stories, humor and impromptu live music. It is located in a circa 1881 building on the Public Square.

North Georgia College & State University also makes available to the public a variety of programs, including plays, musical recitals and concerts.

## LOCAL VINEYARDS AND WINERIES

Although James Edward Oglethorpe was generally unsuccessful in his eighteenth-century attempts to introduce European viticulture into the new colony of Georgia, vintners today are competent in growing European grapes, French-American hybrids and Native American muscadines that produce exceptional wines. Vineyards are now located near Savannah, Statesboro and Albany in the southern part of the state; in Dahlonega, Young Harris and Ringgold in north Georgia, and everywhere in between.

Within the last decade, Lumpkin County has been found to have the perfect climate and soil combination for both European and American wine grapes. The county is widely known as "the heart of Georgia wine country" and is currently the home of numerous vineyards and wineries. All of them offer wine tastings in beautiful settings, complemented by a variety of events, festivals, cuisines and entertainment.

Three Sisters Vineyards was established in 1996 as the first family farm winery in the Frogtown district. The 184-acre former cattle farm was planted with 10,000 European and American wine grapes in 1998, and winery operations began in 2000. Annual production is about 3,500 cases. Founders Sharon and Doug Paul note that Three Sisters is Lumpkin County's first legal commercial producer since Prohibition. It was named "Best Winery in the South" by the Turner South network. The tasting room features colorful Southern folk art and pottery as well as a scenic view of the Three Sisters Mountains.

Frogtown Cellars, a fifty-seven-acre vineyard and winery estate, is home to over 20,000 grape vines and fifteen different varieties of red and white grapes, producing over 180 tons of premium wine grapes per harvest. It was established in 1998 by Cydney and Craig Kritzer, who divided the land into separate vineyards and planted grape varieties based on the characteristics of each site. The tri-level gravity flow winery is located in an impressive cypress timber frame wine tasting and event facility that is noted for its premium wines, event functions and hospitality.

Wolf Mountain Vineyards and Winery was established in 1999 by Linda and Karl Boegner. A 7,500-square-foot gravity flow winery was completed in the spring of 2001. Annual production is about 2,000 cases. The winery estate offers a unique setting for special events, including weddings, receptions, private parties, Sunday brunch and gourmet dinners. Wolf Mountain wines are produced from 100 percent Georgia-grown grapes, hand-picked at the 1,800-foot elevations of the Dahlonega Plateau. The winemaking philosophy is focused on blending varietals to create new and unique wines.

Blackstock Vineyards was founded by David Harris, a twenty-year pioneer in Georgia winemaking. He and his wife Trish spent a decade developing their vineyard and estate winery. Harris's winemaking honors include the first gold medals ever awarded for Georgia-grown white vinifera, red vinifera and the first "Best Southeastern Wine." Blackstock Vineyards is currently Georgia's largest 100 percent vinifera planting. It is located in the Town Creek section of White County, adjacent to Lumpkin's Frogtown district. Winery operations began in 2005.

These Vidal Blanc wine grapes were grown in Lumpkin County and photographed shortly before the 2005 harvest. *Courtesy of Gail Stewart, Cherokee Photo Club.*

It is interesting to observe how Lumpkin County's agribusiness has changed over the years. Cotton, wheat and corn were the major crops grown in the nineteenth century. In the early 1920s the boll weevil put an end to growing cotton, and more corn took its place as the main ingredient in making moonshine. A farmer could make many more gallons an acre than he could bushels!

By this time, however, the land had become depleted of its nutrients from overcultivation and a farmer could barely eke ten to fifteen bushels of corn per acre. The advent of the poultry industry was a great boon in providing free fertilizer to enrich the soil. Chicken houses replaced most row crops on many farms and gave the land a needed rest. Today, vineyards are rapidly becoming a major part of Lumpkin County's agribusiness.

## LEGENDARY GOLD MINE SHAFT DISCOVERED UNDER THE SMITH HOUSE IN 2006

One of the most popular stories told over the years about Dahlonega's Smith House is that it sits atop a rich vein of gold. An item published in an 1899 issue of the *Dahlonega Nugget* reported, "Capt. Hall's workmen while excavating the cellar for his new ware house…struck a rich gold bearing vein several feet wide, depth not known." Editor W.B. Townsend went on to note that Captain Hall had personally informed him that he would not develop the vein, since it ran under his building and was on a town lot.

Other sources say that the city fathers would not allow Hall to mine gold on his property because it was too close to the Public Square and that it was only after losing a six-month legal battle that Hall reluctantly covered up the gold vein. Ironically, after completing the elegant new building designed to be his residence and office, Frank W. Hall and his wife Esther moved away to Ingleside near Atlanta, where Hall died a few months later from typhoid fever. He was only fifty-six, but his obituary described him as "the richest person in Lumpkin County long before he decided to take up his new place of abode."

After housing various businesses during the next two decades, the building was purchased in 1922 by Ben and Bessie Smith, who opened a hotel and restaurant known as the Smith House. Back then, room and board was $1.50 a day. As word spread about Bessie Smith's delicious home cooking, it wasn't long before she had to hire kitchen help to help her cook and serve the meals, which cost all of 35¢ for those not staying at the Smith House.

Ben Smith continued to run the Smith House for a few years after Bessie passed away in 1939 but later sold it to William Manning Smith in 1944. Attorney Will Smith (not related to Ben) had been a member of the defense team that defended Leo M. Frank in the highly publicized Mary Phagan rape and murder case in Atlanta. Two years later Will and Mary Lou Baker Smith sold the entire Smith House block to William B. Fry.

Bill Fry was the son of a gold miner who came to Dahlonega in the late 1800s to be superintendent of the Crown Mountain Mining Company. Fry enjoyed prospecting for gold and frequently took Smith House guests on tours of local mines. He also taught them how to pan for gold. It was Bill Fry's keen interest in gold that led him to become largely responsible for the development of Dahlonega's first gold museum, located on Crown Mountain.

Remodeling recently uncovered a legendary mine shaft in the basement of this 1899 building, which has been home to the Smith House since 1922. *Courtesy of Chris Welch.*

Finding himself with more to do than he had time for, Bill Fry hired Fred Welch to manage the Smith House dining room and kitchen. Fred and his wife Thelma served three meals a day, seven days a week for nearly twenty-five years before turning the business over to their son Freddy and his wife Shirley. The Welch family purchased the Smith House in 1970 and have been operating it successfully ever since.

In February of 2006, the Welches (including son Chris and daughter Freida) began major renovations to the Smith House. While tearing out the floor of the basement to create new restrooms, a worker punched through the concrete to empty space underneath. When the remainder of the concrete had been removed, a large round deep hole was revealed. Word soon spread that Captain Hall's fabled gold mine had been found, and reporters from newspapers and television stations traveled to Dahlonega to see it for themselves and report the exciting news.

After removing ten feet of debris (including handmade bricks, pieces of pottery and many bottles) with a hoist and bucket, the Welches determined the depth of the shaft to be about thirty-two feet. Although there was no horizontal tunnel going off from the shaft, there was an eight-foot wall of quartz about three feet wide. Eager to find out whether or not the quartz was gold bearing, the Welches lowered a workman with a pick to break off pieces of the rock. A bucket filled with roughly two gallons of rock was taken to the Consolidated Gold Mine, where it was crushed into a fine powder. When it was panned by guides there, the crushed ore yielded enough gold to fill a small vial about a quarter full. The story about a gold mine under the Smith House was no longer a legend but a reality.

In addition to the mine shaft, workmen tearing out the old concrete floor found another source of great interest: the rock foundation of some previous building. An intriguing reference in an unidentified old newspaper clipping says that "Free Jim" Bosclair—the former African American slave described in the first chapter—"had a house where the Smith House is now located." After gaining his freedom, James Bosclair came to Dahlonega from Augusta early in the gold rush and reportedly operated a large general merchandise store, an icehouse, stable and saloon. These establishments were located on the lot across the street from where the building that is now the Smith House was built in 1899. Could the recently discovered stacked rock foundation have been part of Bosclair's home? Research is currently being done to determine previous owners of the lot.

Amid all the excitement, the Welches continue with their remodeling plans but with one major change: they plan to cover the mine shaft with plexiglass to enable visitors to see for themselves how Dahlonega's history is still making itself known in the present.

# Afterword

As the reader may have inferred from learning about local history still in the making, Dahlonega has been growing by leaps and bounds, especially in the past decade. Georgia Highway 400 provides a direct route from Atlanta to Dahlonega unlike the narrow winding roads of the past. Many people make the daily commute to work in Atlanta in order to live in this vibrant community nestled in the foothills of the Blue Ridge Mountains.

The population includes many retirees, who came to visit and stayed to live. The number of people living in town is rapidly approaching five thousand, with new people moving in every day. The county population grew 44 percent in the decade between 1990 and 2000 and has grown 25 percent in the past four years. It is now conservatively estimated at twenty-five thousand.

Dahlonega welcomes new faces, ideas and talents, even as it works to maintain the quality of life that draws people to come here. Old-timers and newcomers alike volunteer their time and energy to implement numerous projects to preserve and enhance the community.

Winston Churchill once observed, "The farther backward you can look, the farther forward you are likely to see." The community called Dahlonega incorporates the wisdom of Churchill's words in its efforts to achieve a balanced perspective of past, present and future. It continues to preserve and celebrate its colorful history while simultaneously planning for and managing the growth that is an inevitable part of being an active and proactive community.

# Bibliography

Amerson, Anne Dismukes. *The Best of "I Remember Dahlonega."* Charleston: The History Press, 2006.

———. *Dahlonega's Historic Public Square: Then & Now Stories about the Buildings and the People.* Dahlonega, GA: Chestatee Publications, 2002.

———. *I Remember Dahlonega: Memories of Growing Up in Lumpkin County,* Volumes 1–4. Dahlonega, GA: Chestatee Publications, 1990–97.

———. *A North Georgia Journal of History: A Thirty-Two County Compendium of Historic Information Related to the North Georgia Region,* Volumes 24. Compiled and Edited by Olin Jackson. Roswell, GA: Legacy Communications, Inc., 1991-1999.

Amerson, Anne Dismukes, and Kate Cassady Brehe. *Screen & Stage: The Story of Dahlonega's Historic Holly Theatre.* Dahlonega, GA: The Holly Theatre Community Center, Inc., 2003.

Anthony, Jack. "Dahlonega: A Special Place." Dahlonega, GA: self-published, 2000.

Bragg, William Harris. *Joe Brown's Army: The Georgia State Line, 1862–1865.* Macon, GA: Mercer University Press, 1987.

Cain, Andrew W. *History of Lumpkin County for the First Hundred Years 1832–1932.* Spartanburg, SC: The Reprint Company, 1984.

Ehle, John. *Trail of Tears: The Rise and Fall of the Cherokee Nation.* New York: Anchor Books / Doubleday, 1988.

Head, Sylvia Gailey, and Elizabeth W. Etheridge. *The Neighborhood Mint: Dahlonega in the Age of Jackson.* Macon, GA: Mercer University Press, 1986.

Lange, David W. *History of the United States Mint and Its Coinage.* Atlanta: Whitman Publishing, 2005.

O'Kelley, Harold Ernest. *Dahlonega's Blue Ridge Rangers in the Civil War, 1863–1865.* Gainesville, GA: Georgia Printing Company, 1992.

# Bibliography


Roberts, William Pittman. *Georgia's Best Kept Secret: A History of North Georgia College.* Dahlonega, GA: William P. Roberts and the Alumni Association of North Georgia College, 1998.

Sorohan, Sallie. "Gold Rush Days in Dahlonega: the History of a Mountain Festival." Dahlonega, GA: self-published, 2002.

Spencer, Emma Dill Russell. *Green Russell and Gold.* Austin: University of Texas Press, 1966.

Williams, David. *The Georgia Gold Rush: Twenty-Niners, Cherokees, and Gold Fever.* Columbia: University of South Carolina Press, 1993.

Winter, Douglas. *Gold Coins of the Dahlonega Mint, 1838–1861.* Dallas: DWN Publishing, 1997.

Yeates, W.S., S.W. McCallie, and Francis P. King. *A Preliminary Report on a Part of the Gold Deposits of Georgia.* Geological Survey of Georgia Bulletin No. 4-A, 1896. Reprint, Atlanta: Geologic Survey Branch of the Environmental Protection Division of the Georgia Department of Natural Resources, 1989.

# Index

## J



## K



## L



## M



## N



## O



## P



## Q

## R



## S



## T



## W



## Y

Printed in the USA
CPSIA information can be obtained
at www.ICGtesting.com
LVHW081934061023
760333LV00024B/36

9 781540 204103